This Companion is the second book in the series and is designed as a resource to help improve your repertoire on the B Flat Flute. I have included the same tutorial and introduction to the instrument from the previous book in case the buyer doesn't have a copy of the first book but none of the tunes have been reprinted here.

Stuart Boyd

Stafford

UK

Printed in the UK by Lulu.com

ISBN: 978-1-4716-0391-4

To assist students with understanding the abc notation, all tunes will be available on Youtube at the following address,

www.youtube.com/user/accordionstu

Welcome to the second book of tunes for B Flat Flute.

This is a collection of 200 tunes which include those played by many flute bands across the UK and Ireland. The tunes include traditional melodies and folk ballads from different communities across the UK. The intention is to harness a wide selection of tunes which are popular in this era and present them in a simple 'abc' music format, popular with most flute bands.

There wasn't anything on the market to satisfy the demands of Fluter's who don't read music and most students learning the B Flat flute would have to join a band and gather tunes this way.

The internet has a few decent sites which post flute notes free as I do myself but after the success of the first 'B Flat Fluter's Companion' in 2008, people have asked for a bigger book with more tunes that they can have a source of reference to carry around with them or keep on the bookshelf at home.

I later improved some aspects of the book, including changing the font to something which is more DDA compliant, included a better finger chart and in response to some people buying the first book, then contacting me and asking where they can buy a B Flat Flute from, I have included those makers who I know and respect.

I will be uploading all the tunes to Youtube for those who aren't familiar with how the tune should sound. Building the tune archive on Youtube is on going.

www.stuartboyd.co.uk

Joining a Band

If you are fortunate enough to have a band that rehearses locally, you should think about joining them as you will benefit from the experience of all their members and most likely get one to one tutoring.

When you join a band you are likely to get one of their flutes to help you learn the tunes. Some bands give learners their worst flutes, with keys held together with elastic bands and electrical tape this is sad as it only delays the progress of the student and if you are serious about learning the flute I would recommend buying your own instrument if you can afford it. It would be useful to discuss this with a senior member of the band first and make sure you buy the same type of flute.

There are quite a few different flutes on the market today and most have slight differences in tuning which can be heard by the trained ear and it's best to play the same instrument as the band you join.

Among flute bands there are different genres to wet everyone's appetite. **Blood & Thunder** bands play traditional Loyalist tunes and novelty or party tunes in a very energetic, loud and fun style. Some Blood & Thunder bands mix singing in with some of their tunes and it isn't unusual to see the band members snaking from side to side, down the road. The digital age has benefitted the flute band scene hugely with the majority of bands now posting clips of their parades on video sharing sites such as Youtube and Vimeo.

This has helped more people gain access to the flute band scene from all over over the world and it is a valuable place for bands to post their new tunes and their members can practice along, at home in front of the computer.

Computer games and game consoles such as X Box and PlayStations and cult Japanese Anime cartoons have also left their mark on flute band music in regards to the catchy theme tunes on most of their games. This book wouldn't be representative of the flute band scene today if it didn't include some of these tunes. Super Mario brothers, Family Guy, Game of Thrones, Yakumo's Theme are just a few that are included.

Melody bands play some tunes that Blood & Thunder bands play but they also add a repertoire of military marches and have parts written for second and third flutes with members playing counter melodies parallel to the main tune and sometimes F Bass flutes and a Piccolo chirping high above the melodies. **Melody** bands attract musicians who take the music a little more seriously with a greater emphasis on hitting the right notes, played the correct way and reading music by dots is essential, especially for those playing parts.

Corps of Drums bands are similar to melody bands but they tend to model the bands identity on ex regiments of the British Army. They wear replica uniforms and play mainly military marches and every tune will be arranged into different parts. Corps of Drums also have Buglers which isn't a common site in bands in N.Ireland and the drummers can have an array of tenor drums, snare drums, rope tension drums as well as a bass drum instead of the usual snare & Bass drums which most bands have.

36th Ulster Division Regimental Band U.V.F

If there are a few bands in your area and you are not sure which one to join, go to one of their competitions and watch them perform, you will get a better feel for the band and help you decide which one is right for you.

The important thing to remember is that joining a band isn't just like joining the youth club, you are being welcomed into a family of people who will support you through your initial learning and for many years afterwards. Being a member of a band is a two way relationship, you will need to commit your time to their engagements and take an active role in fundraising for new instruments and uniforms and in return you will be a proud member of the band whilst being a living part of our culture.

Looking after your flute

As stated earlier in the book, there are a few different types of flutes on the market made from a variety of materials and cleaning and caring for the type of flute you have will depend on which material it is made from.

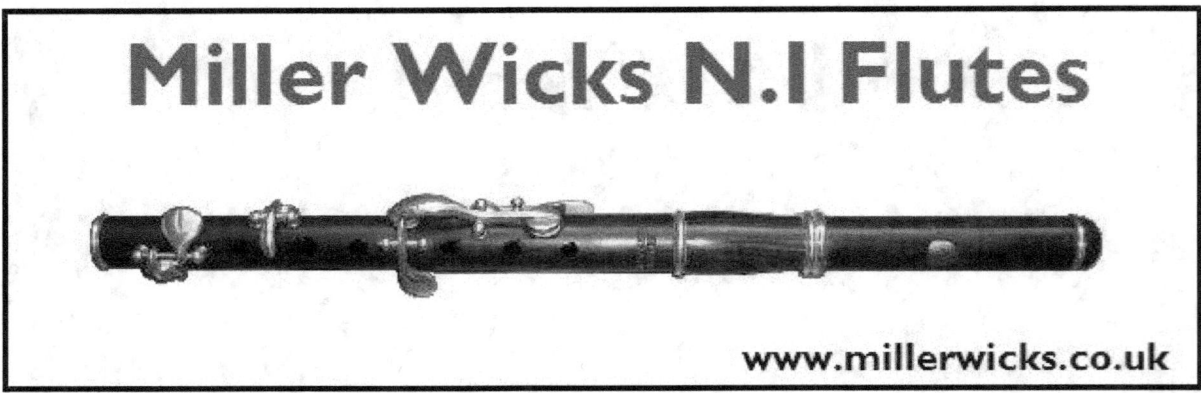

Miller Wicks N.I Flutes

www.millerwicks.co.uk

Wooden Flutes

Miller Wicks, Millyard -Molem, Peter Worrell, Mullan, Mull Wilks, Crown AZ's, Ruddal and Carte and Potters are the main types of wooden flutes that I have come across over the past 25 years.

They are all made out of African Blackwood or similar Blackwood's and although it has a good level of moisture resistance, being wood it will dry out in warmer climates and at higher ambient temperatures. African Blackwood or Mopingo is harvested at an unsustainable rate and current stock levels are in decline but demand is greater than ever. This will unfortunately reflect on the price of flutes in the future unless a different wood is used such as cocobolo or rosewood.

A wooden flute will take a few months of regular playing to settle properly. The process is called 'Blown in' and it just means that the pads will settle to make a good seal over the holes ,the cork will settle to ensure a good seal and the inner bore of the flute body will season and sound better etc.

 It is advisable to clean your wooden flute with oil on a regular basis. I clean my flute once a week and use a small amount of linseed oil soaked onto a cotton ball. Just rub the oil over the body flute and between the keys but don't get any oil on the pads. Oil the head joint too and rub the oil into the wood for a good five minutes.

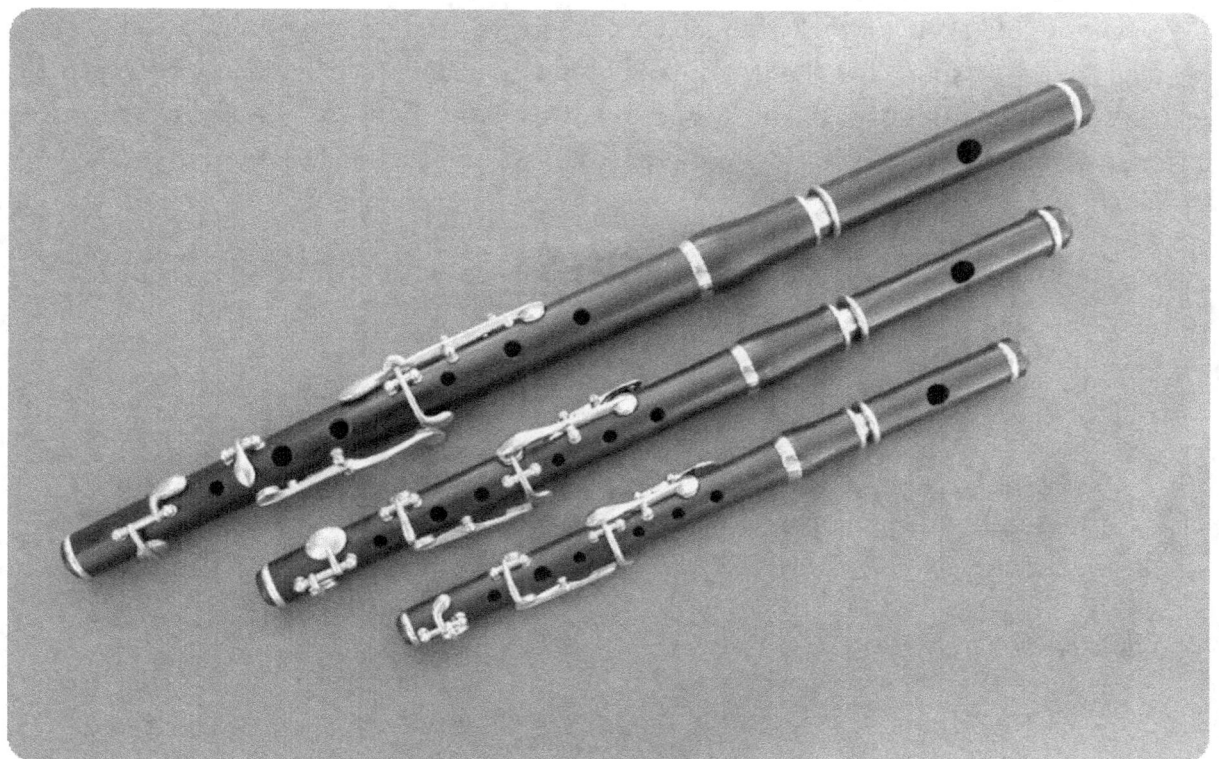

The Family of Millyard Molem Flutes

I then take the flute in a cloth rag or duster and use a simple pull through with a small screw tied on one end of a piece of cord and a small strip of cloth soaked in oil, tied to the other end.

Remove the head joint from the body of the flute so that the flute is in two halves, then drop the screw down the inside of the body and let it drop out of the bottom. Then gently pull the screw and the cord and the oil soaked strip of cloth will be dragged down the barrel, cleaning the inside of any spit residue and it will soak into the wood making it water resistant for a short period of time.

Linseed Oil is fine on wood but the leather pads don't like oil at all, so I fold a small piece of newspaper the size of a postage stamp in half and tuck it underneath the key pads to stop any oil settling on the pads, you could even fold a small square of tin foil around the pad when oiling the flute.

The inside of the head joint is cleaned by using a thin piece of wood or pencil and ram rodding a small cotton ball with a little oil down to just under the embouchure hole and then pulling it back and forth a few times to clean and coat the inside of the head joint.

Currently Peter Worrell, Mullan Flutes and Millyard-Molem flutes include a cleaning rod and cork grease when you purchase a new instrument from them and I believe Miller Wicks will be doing this soon as well.

Care needs to be taken not to disturb the cork otherwise you may send your instrument off key and you won't sound like the rest of the flutes in the band. An experienced band captain will be able to tune this back relatively quickly and all flutes should be checked and tuned before a parade to ensure there are no surprises on parade especially in front of judges.

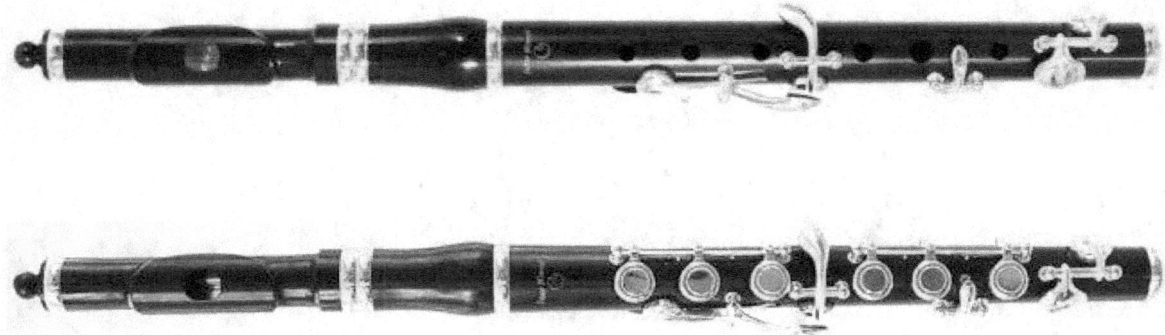

Two flutes from Peter Worrell

The cork should be left alone and never allow the head to be knowingly immersed in water. Water will put stresses on the cork and pads and will affect the sound of the flute.

When not playing the flute it should be stored away from heat or damp, never leave one on a radiator or window sill or even on the back shelf of the car as they will dry out quicker than you think and if the instrument gets warped then its no use to you anymore.

If you do notice any cracks in your flute, don't try to repair them yourself. There are some very skilled instrument makers amongst our community and all those mentioned earlier will be able to repair your flute professionally. A bad repair can make the crack worse.

If you don't already have a flute case for storage, visit some of the websites listed in the back of the book and enquire whether they have any for sale. Protecting your flute will keep it in good order for many years and if you do decide to part with it for a different type, you will get a fairer price if it's been well looked after.

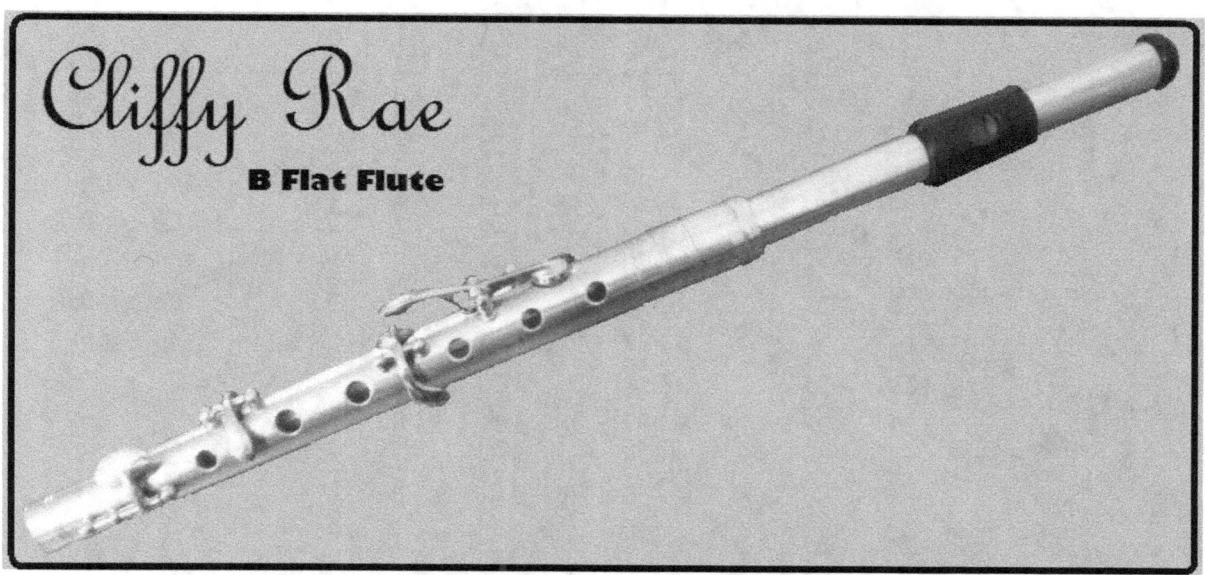

Metal Flutes

The only one that I am aware of at the moment is the Cliffy Rae flute. There have been a few models from Clifford Rae over the years and his latest model is a fine instrument.

Being metal it is hard wearing and doesn't require much maintenance except to clean the inside with a cotton ball after playing. Unlike a wooden flute it isn't porous and doesn't require oiling or polish. The Metal flutes are anodised and are totally waterproof. The head joint is one piece and is attached to the flute by a tenon with two or three rubber O-rings which help make a perfect air seal.

It is important to remove the head joint as soon as you get your flute and apply a little amount of Vaseline or silicone grease to the o rings to enable the head joint to be removed easily each time.

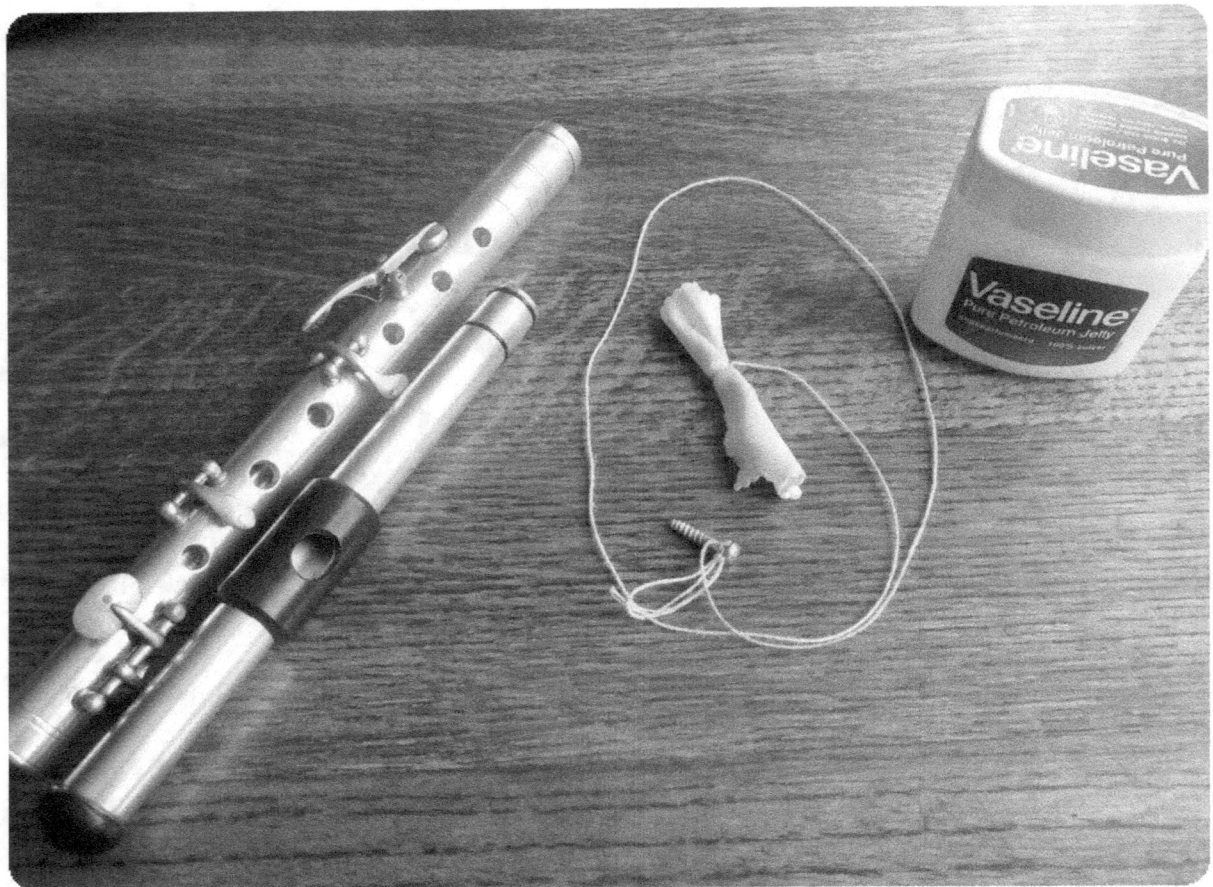

The cork in the Cliffy Rae is made of hard plastic and is less likely to suffer from the same issues as a proper cork but you should still take care when cleaning. The embouchure is enclosed in a plastic raised lip plate which is handy especially in cold weather.

I have heard tales from band members that metal flutes tend to seize up in very cold weather and I could only advise that you keep the instrument close to your flesh and keep it warm before playing it on a cold day parade.

As the instrument is impervious to most other issues that the wooden flute suffers from, I feel that these flutes will be with us for a long time.

Plastic Flutes

It sounds horrible but flutes made out of Ebonite, a type of vulcanised hard rubber or Bakelite, the world's first synthetic plastic have been around since the 1930's with varying successes.

Rudall & Rose made a few decent models of B Flat and F Flutes in Bakelite and today there are Miller Browne's, Browne Wicks, Crossett's, Ferris, Drum sounds etc. Many of these are made in factories in India or China and with few exceptions they lack the quality and consistency of the makers of wooden and metal flutes.

In my opinion the best of these types on the market is the well-established Miller Browne flute. Not only because it has been around for over 30 years but spares can be purchased inexpensively and they are readily available.

Made from Ebonite it is water resistant inside and out and needs little maintenance except to be cleaned with a little oil on the inside and light brush against the base of the keys to get rid of dead skin and spray with a little lukewarm soapy water on the outside and cleaned with a cotton ball.

The head joint should be treated as the wooden head joint and the pull thru can be used on the Miller Browne too.

Again if you can buy a simple case for your flute, they can be bought second hand on ebay at the moment for a tenner alternatively use a long card tube used to send posters in the mail, they can be bought from the stationer for a couple of quid at the maximum.

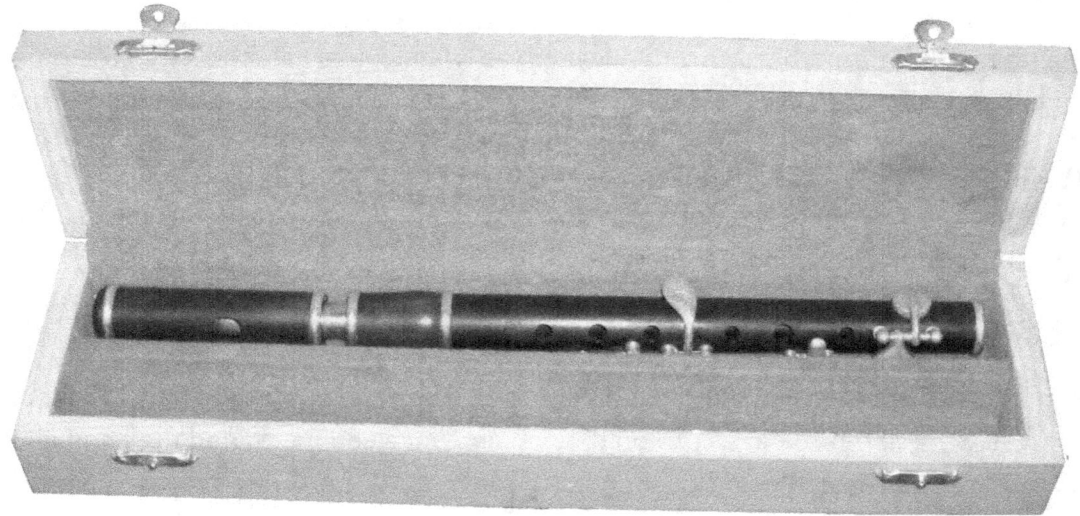

Learning to play the Flute

I would recommend asking a flute player to play your flute before you even try, this is to make sure that it doesn't have any defects. If they can play all the notes easily then you won't be able to make excuses and blame the flute later.

It isn't easy to blow the flute otherwise everyone would be playing them, it takes patience and control and a lot of practice to be able to get the notes sounding as they should do and if you follow the next few steps you will be on the right path to mastering the blowing technique.

Step1 – Remove the head joint.

It is easier to get the first note out of the flute by blowing into the head joint alone. Place the head joint between both hands and place the embouchure hole directly under the middle of your bottom lip.

There is a recess between most peoples lip and chin and the contour of the head joint fits nicely into this recess. You shouldn't have to press it hard against your flesh and relax your grip so that you can concentrate on your tongue.

Step 2 – Dry Spit

Once you are ready, inhale enough air to fill your lungs about ¾ full and imagine there is a small piece of tobacco in the middle and at the edge of your bottom lip, You are going to try to blow this piece of tobacco off your lip and down into the embouchure hole. The secret however is not to spit a gobfull of saliva all over the place when doing it.

Practice doing this in front of a mirror and watch as when you exhale the air a little hole opens between your lips, this should be a very small hole and shouldn't sound too breathy.

Try dry spitting for a split second and listen out for a noise that sounds like a flute. Keep doing this until you can hear the noise and you may need to twist the head joint slightly to get the right sound. Once you have mastered this move on.

Step 3 – Replace the body of the flute

At first don't try covering any holes, just hold the flute as before with one hand on either end as if you were about to eat a corn on the cob and once you have lined the head joint up again, try dry spitting into the embouchure hole again.

You might be a little frustrated that it is more difficult than before and this is because the tube that you are trying to fill with air has got longer and it will take a little more effort to be able to reach the note.

Keep practising this until you can do it by picking the flute up and blowing the note first time. The note you are trying to hit is called C sharp (C#).

If you are struggling, remove the head joint and go back to Step1 and keep going until you have got it. This can be achieved within a day or could take some people weeks depending on the muscles in their mouth and breath control.

Step 4 – Hold it properly

Once you have mastered the first note you can have a go at holding the flute properly. The thumb on your left hand should be placed parallel to the top of the first hole and the three fingers on your left hand should be resting beside the first three holes. Your little finger will hover over the G# key.

The thumb of your right hand should rest underneath the 4th hole with the three fingers resting at the side of the next three holes. The little finger should be resting on top of, but not pressing with any force on top of the bottom key (D#)

Lift the flute up and line up the head joint as earlier and try to dry spit c# again. If this is achievable then you could try covering the first hole with your left index finger and you should hear a sound which relates to the note B.

At the back of the book you will see a finger chart for all the notes you will need for most tunes. I would advise starting with low d and working your way across each page until you can play all the notes properly and easily before moving on to learning your first tune.

Learning the first tune

The first tune I learned and most people learn in flute bands is the national anthem. The beauty about learning the B Flat Flute is that most of the traditional tunes we play in the bands are tunes that we know and either whistle or sing the melodies long before we even play them. The tunes are part of our culture and we have the benefit over other musicians in that we know what the tune should sound like and once we have the notes in front of us, we don't need to know how long to hold the note for or whether it should be played this way or that way, we should be able to play it from our own memories.

Playing by ear is a skill and one that amazes other musicians and non-musicians in other parts of the world, but it feels normal to most bandsmen and women in our own culture and that is one of the traits that makes us unique.

There are of course many tunes which are more difficult to learn by ear and be able to recall as easily especially marches and tunes which have multiple parts arranged, these parts can be unrecognisable as being part of the tune when played on their own and it is with the rest of the band that they come to life and don't sound great to whistle to either.

As we have already decided that we know how the tune should sound, we support this by using a simple abc system instead of having to learn how to read music. In hindsight I wish that I had learned to read music a lot earlier in my musical career as the abc system has a limitation but it is still the preferred method of learning simple tunes quickly for most flute bands today.

The system I use in the previous B Flat Fluters Companion is the same one that I use in this book.

All low notes are in lower case, all notes in the middle register are in capitals and all high notes have a ' beside the capital.

National Anthem – God Save Our Queen

GGAF#GA BBCBAG

AGF#G GABC

D'D'D'D'CB CCCCBA

BCBAG BCD'

E'D' CB A G

Using this method for tunes which we know the words for, each note is played at the same time as the syllable would be said in the song eg.

God Save Our Gra Cious Queen

G   G   A   F#   G   A

Practice, Practice, Practice.

Once you have learned your first tune, practice the hell out of it, play it alongside other fluters too as it is different than playing on your own in the house.

I would recommend practising between 20 -30 mins per day, otherwise your mouth muscles get slack and you won't be able to reach and maintain those high notes for any length of time.

Once you get into the flow, you will be learning a tune a day easily. The only thing that restricts most Fluter's repertoire is their reluctance to step outside of their own little political sphere and try to play tunes which may presently be associated with one community or another.

I am constantly searching for different tunes to keep my interest and some of them are included in this book, influences from Italian folk music, Irish Rebel and Loyalist tunes, Chinese folk tunes and Welsh folk tunes.

Accessories

Most flute makers and suppliers now supply some accessories within the price when purchasing a new instrument.

Peter Worrell Flutes come with a Faux Drawstring bag for the coronet flutes and a more substantial pouch for the Crown Flutes. They also include a Cork grease stick and a metal cleaning rod along with makers advice and tips on looking after your flute.

Millyard Molem Flutes include a well made cloth roll with crok grease, spare tennon cotton and a cleaning rod with a pre-marked line to help measure where the tuning cork should be. Tony has included a valuable information leaflet on how to care for your flute.

Mullan Flutes come in a durable flute case and also have a cleaning rod.

Ferris Flutes come in a decent zippable case with a small jewellers screwdriver and a cleaning rod.

Miller Wicks N.I also supply a cleaning rod and cork grease when purchasing a new flute.

Over the next few pages I have included some graphics to help you learn all the notes played on the B Flat Flute

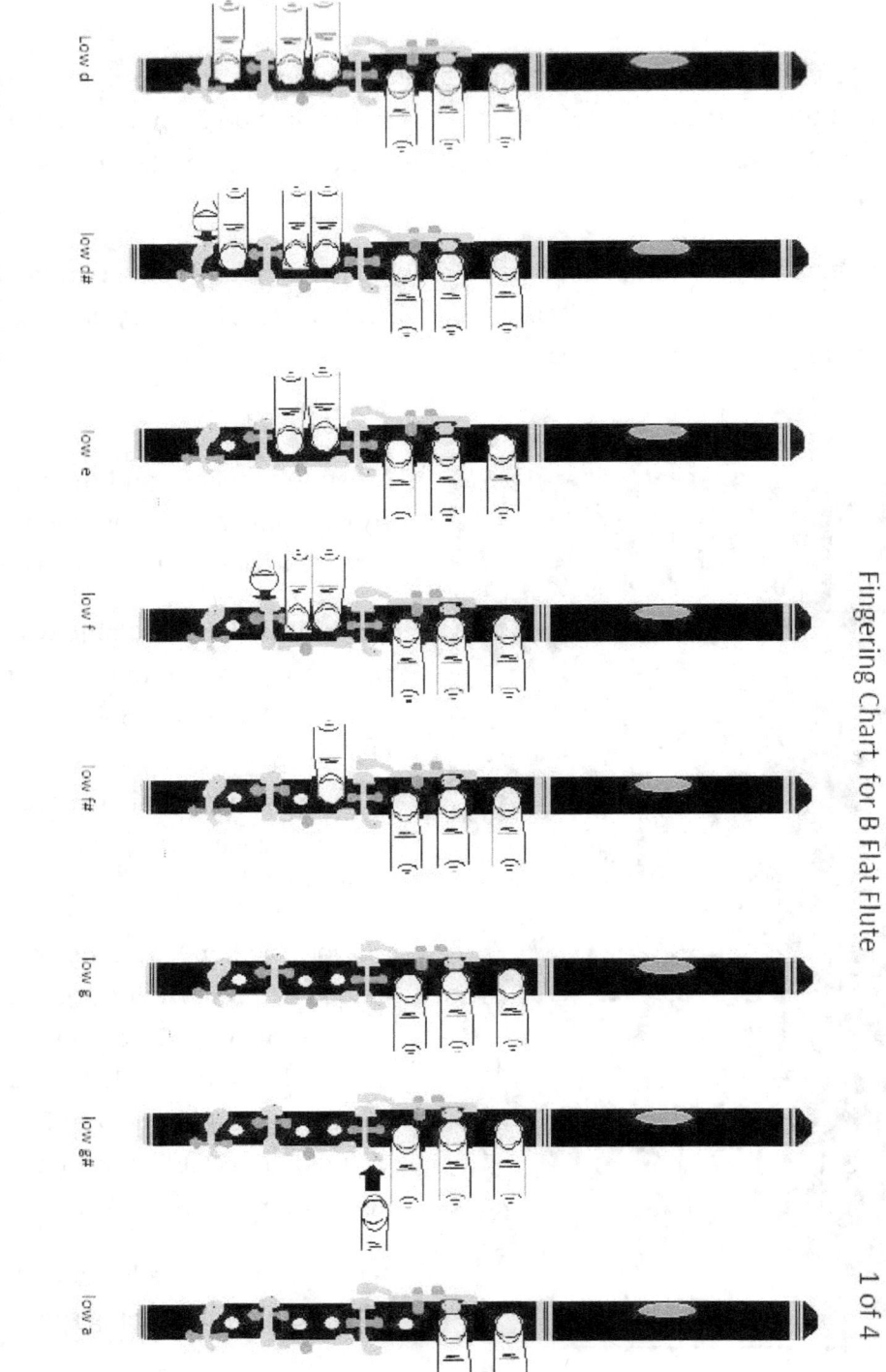

Fingering Chart for B Flat Flute

Illustrated by S. Boyd www.stuartboyd.co.uk

1 of 4

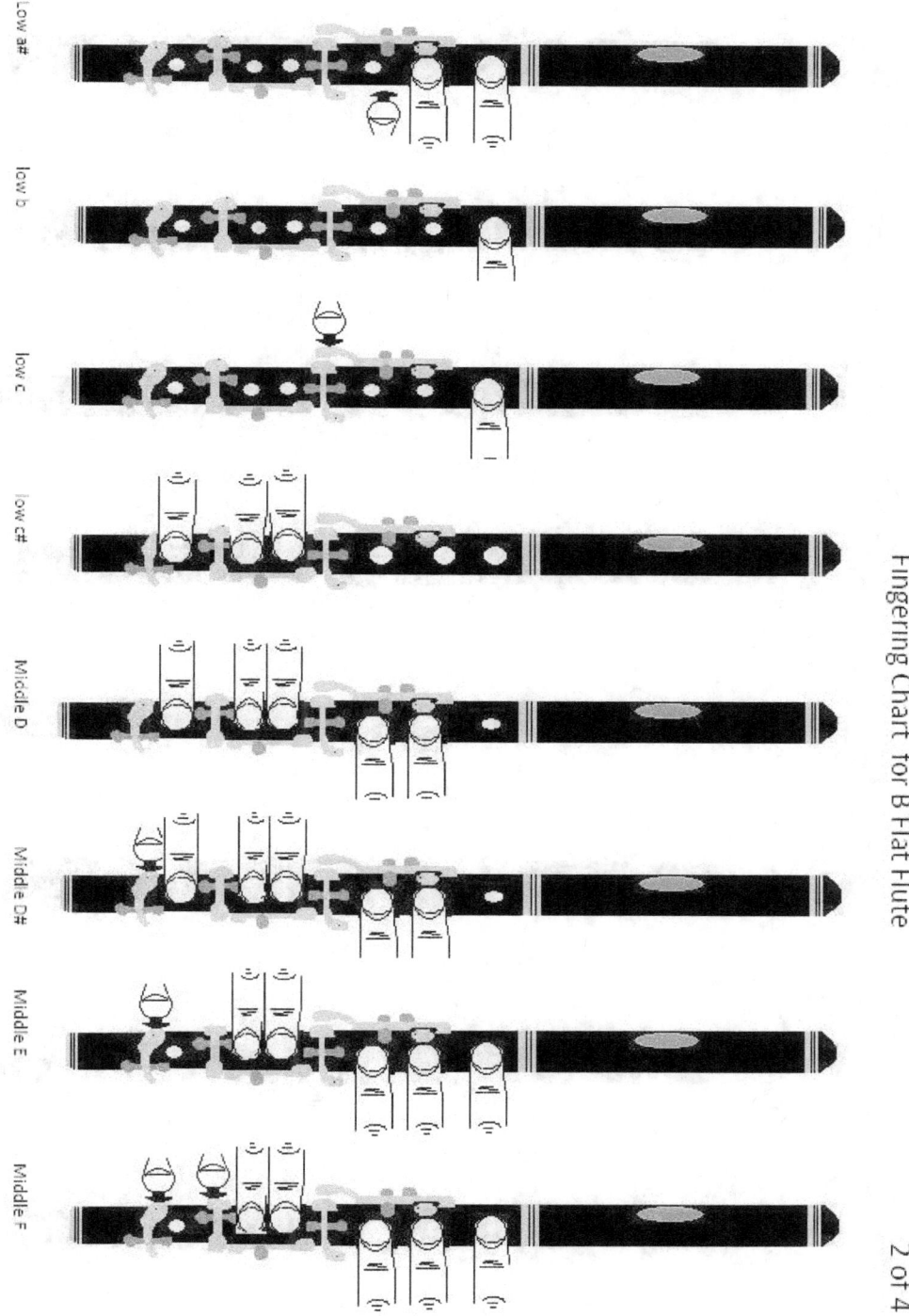

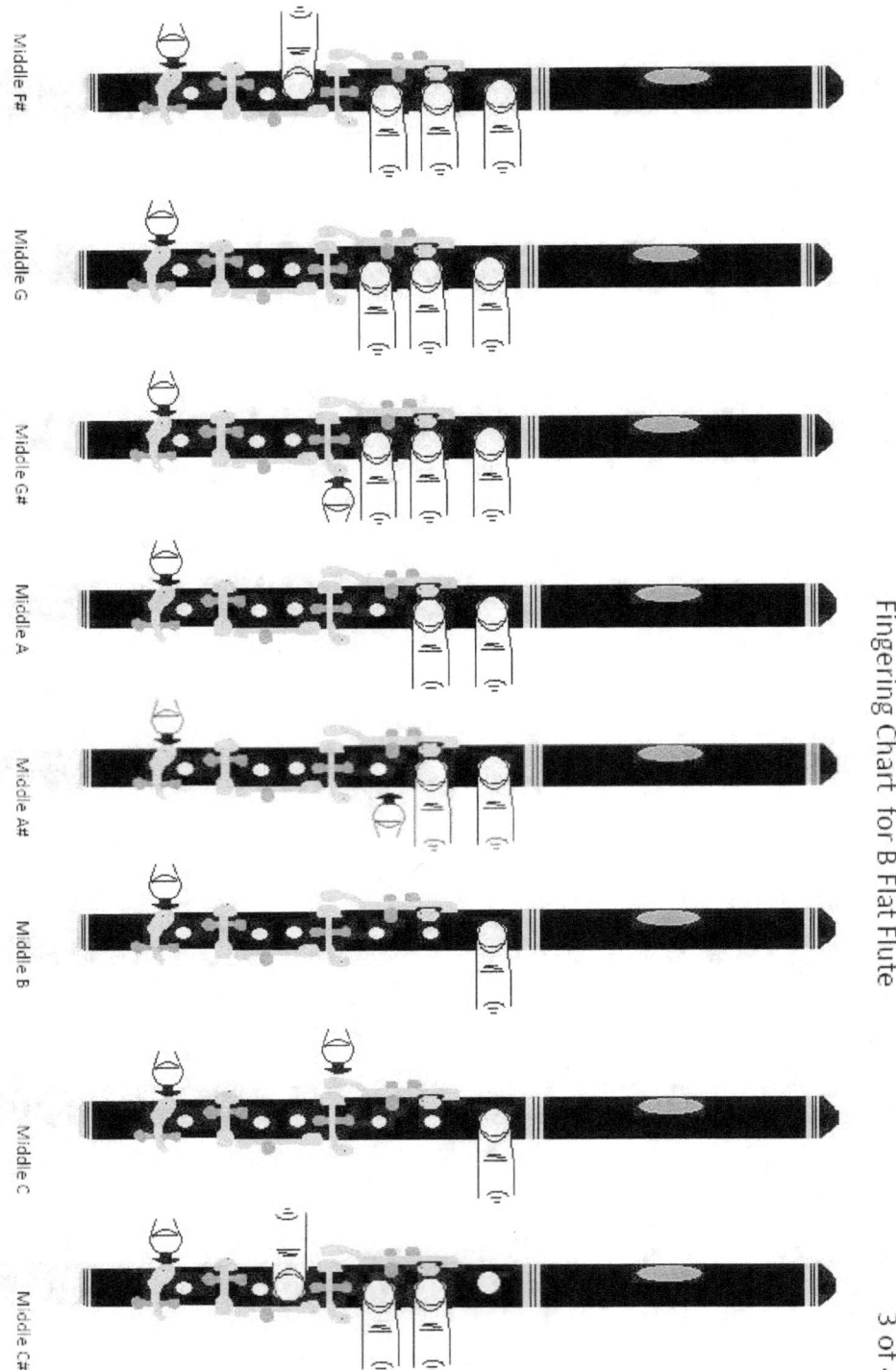

Illustrated by S. Boyd www.stuartboyd.co.uk

Middle F#

Middle G

Middle G#

Middle A

Middle A#

Middle B

Middle C

Middle C#

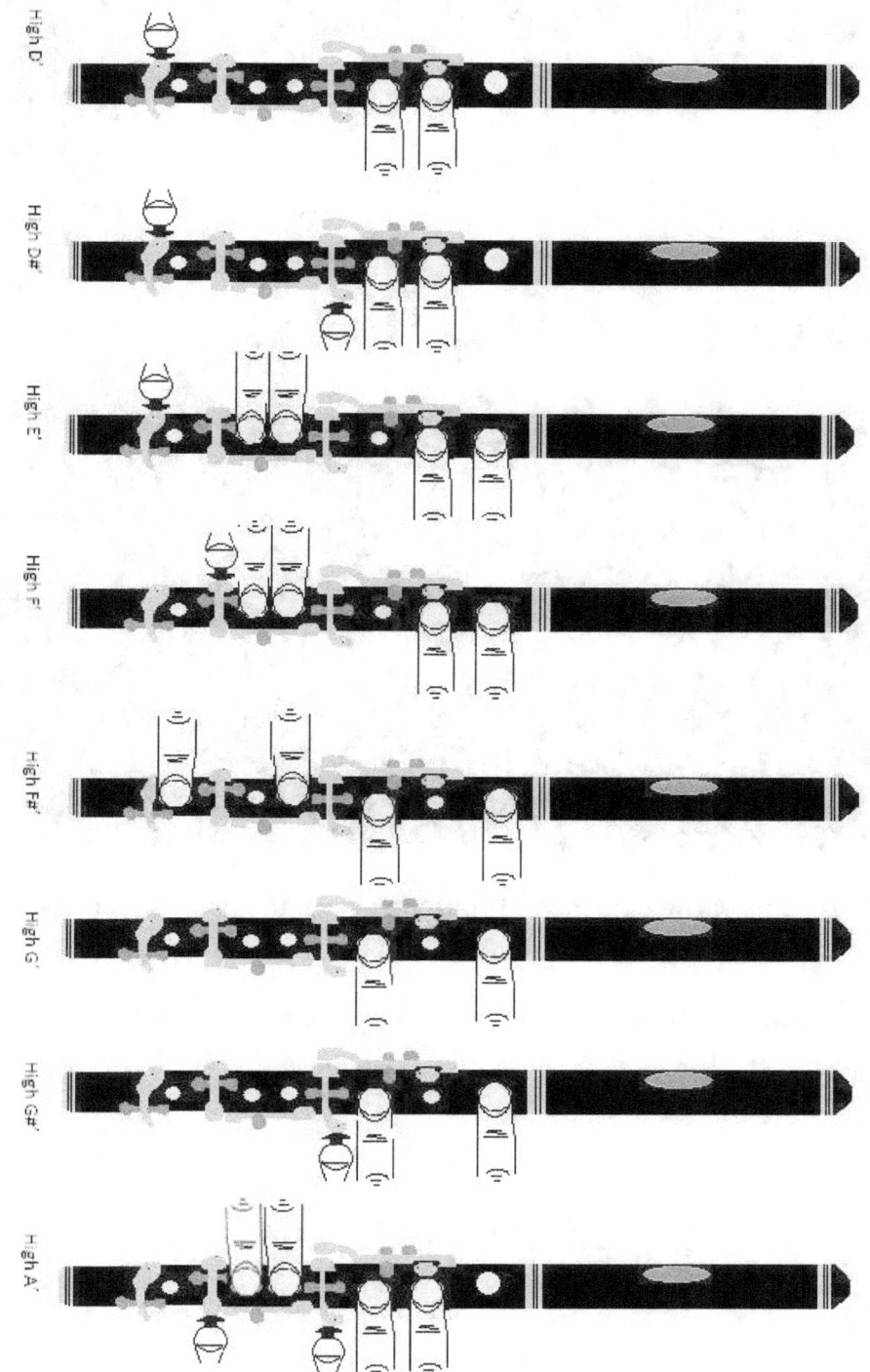

Illustrated by S. Boyd www.stuartboyd.co.uk

Fingering Chart for B Flat Flute

All the tunes in this book will be uploaded to Youtube before the book is published and I will have an Index on my website which links through to each video.

For further support you can contact me through my website or Youtube, just leave me a message.

www.stuartboyd.co.uk

www.youtube.com/user/accordionstu

Tunes Index

Shine Jesus Shine

F#'E'F#'D' G'F#'E'B D'D'C#D'E'

F#'E'F#'D' G'F#'E'E'E'

F#'E'F#'D' G'F#'E'CBD'D'C#D'E'

F#'E'F#'D' G'F#'E'E'D'D'

AABAGA F#EAA AAB AGA F#E AA

BB C# BC#D' AF# BB BBC# BC#D' AF# BB

GF#GE GF#GE F# G A

F#'E'F#'D' G'F#'E'B D'D'C#D'E'

F#'E'F#'D' G'F#'E'E'E'

F#'E'F#'D' G'F#'E'CB D'D'C#D'E'

F#'E'F#'D' G'F#'E'E'D'D'

The Green Green Grass of Home

DDD c# ED DEGGED DGABBBA BCB AGF#A

GB D'D'D' BCBAG GGF#G AGF#ED DG GAAGF#G

GB D'D'D' BCBAG GGF#G AGF#ED DG GAAGF#G

Dalmore

CDE aagabcba AAGA AGEEDcDE cbcD bab

CDE aagabCba AAGA AGE DC b Dbaga

The Lochaber Badger

BAGAGE EDEGDEG

BAGAGE EDGDE

EDEGEGA AGAD'B AGAGE EDGDE

EDEGEGA AGAD'B AGAGE EDGDE

The Sprigs of Kilrea

BA F#GA F#'D'E'D'E'DF#'D'

BAF#GA D' E'D'AF#E

BAF#GA F#'D'E'D'E'F#'D'

AD'E'F#'G'F#'E'F#'D'D'D'

F#G AAAA GF# GGGG

F#EF#F#F#F# EDEAAA

BAF#GA F#'D'E'D'E'F#'D'

AD'E'F#'G'F#'E'F#'D'D'D'

The Murder of McBriars

AGF#D F#A D'C# C#D'E' AC#BA.

AGF#D F#A D' B C#D'C# AB G#A.

AGF# D F#A D'C# C#D'E' A C# BA

AGF# DEF#GG A F#GF# DED

Flower of Castlerock

D GGGGGF#G ABBBBBABCD'D'D'D'DE'D'CBA D'E'D'

D GGGGG F#G ABBBBBABC D'D'D'D'D'E'D' CBAGAG

BCD'BABG AGEF#G DbD GABD' E'D' BAGA ABA

BCD' BABG AGEF#G DbD GABD' E'D' BABG GAG

BCD' BAGG' BCD' BAG G' BCD' BAGG ABBAABA

BCD' BABG AGEF#G DbD GABD'E'D' BAB GGAG

The Eagle

D'D' BAG GE'CBA AA F#ED CCB D' CBAD

D' BAG GE'CBA AA F#ED D' AF#G

D BCB D' BAG AGF#ED E G A BCB AA

D BCB D' BAG AGF#ED EG AGG

Ratclift Cross

GD cDbgE cE ac eaf#d

f#ac bagf#ed D bgf#g d gf#ag

DGBGCBAGF#D cEAE AGF#EDc

bDGD GF#EDcD bgf#g d gf#ag

GD F AGFE cbc A E GBAGF#

Dc#D BF#GBAGF#EDc

bgf#g d gf#ag

BGDGbDGBEc CAEAcEACF#D

Ecace acEF#D bgf#g d gf#ag

NB: This tune has f naturals and f sharps.

North & South

AD'C#D'E'D' ABAGF#E AD' A BAGF#E

AD'C#D'E'D' ABAGF#E AD'D'C#D'E'C#D'

F#'D'A'D' F#' G'F#'E'D' E'C#A C#D'E' F#'G'F#'E'

F#'D'A'D' F#' G'F#'E'D' E'E' F#'G'G'F#'E'D'

Tumbledown

AF#AD' ABC#D' BA AF#AD' F#F# GF#E

AF#A D' ABC#D' BA DEF# AA BA GF#E F#ED

D'BD' G' D'E'F#'G'E'D' D'BD'G' BBCBA

D'BD'G' D'E'F#'G'E'D' GAB D' D'E'D' CBA BAG

GBD' GBD' E'F#'G'E'D' GBD' GBD' BBCBA

GBD' GBD' E'F#'G'E'D' GAB D' D'E'D' CBA BAG

D'BD' G' D'E'F#'G'E'D' D'BD'G' BBCBA

D'BD'G' D'E'F#'G'E'D' GAB D' D'E'D' CBA BAG

White Hackle

D'C#D'E'A F#'E'D'

BAGF# EF#AD' E'F#'A A G'F#'E'D'C#

C#D'E' D'E'F#'E' D'C# BA ABAGF#

BAGF# EF#AD' E'F#'A A G'F#'E'D'C#

C#D'E' D'E'F#'E' F#'G'A F#'E'D'

D'C#D'E'A A E'A A G'F#'E'A A E' F#'G'F#'E'

BAGF# EF#AD' E'F#'A A G'F#'E'D'C#

C#D'E' D'E'F#'E' F#'G'A F#'E'D'

White Gates

AGF#E#F#E#F#AA D' C# BAGF#G F#GF#G BB

E'D'C# BAGF#EF#EF# AA D' C# BAGF#E AAA C#D'

E'E'E' E F# ABA

AD'D' D'C# B C#C# BE C#C# C# BA BAB

ABAF#A D'D' D'C# B C#C# BE EF#G ABABC#D'

D' GB D'E'D' BGF#A CD' CC BD'CBAG ABE'D'

D'GB D'E'D' BGF#A CE' D'C#D'E'D'CBAG

Londonderry on the Foyle

GAB BB GAG E GED

BCD'D'D' BE'D' BGA

G E'E'E' F#' G'G'F#E'D' B

BGA GA BAG EGG

The Knights of St Patrick

Dc#D F#AF# Dc#D af#d gbgf# a f#ef#gab c#

D F#AF# Dc#D af#d gbgf# af#eded

AGA F#DF# ABAAGF#G GEc# ac#EGF#E

AGA F#DF# ABAAF#G AF#D BGE EDc#D

AGA F#DF# ABAAGF#G GEc# ac#EGF#E

D EDE F#EF# GF#G AF#D BGE Daf# d

Borders Edge

D E GG D E G A B A G E B A GG
D E GG D E G A B A G E B A GG

G B D` E' E' D' B A G G' F#' E' E' D' D' B A
D E GG D E G A B A G E B A GG

St Louis Blues

DG DG DED G DG DED GDG DEDG DG DED

G' E'D'CBAG C#D' G'G'G' E'D'CBAG

C#D' G' E'D'CBAG C#D' G'G'G' E'D'CBAG DG

A#BD'BG F# F DEF#G BA# G DRUMS

DEF#G B DEF#G BA# G DRUMS

DF#AF#D c#c DEF#G BA# G

A#BD'BG F# F DEF#G BA#

GGGG BBBB D'D'D'D' G'

DEF#G B DEF#G BA# GGGG GGGG BGED

DF#AF#D c# c DEF#G BA# G DRUMS

BGAB GAA#BG F# BA#BA F# BA#BA#BAF#

AF#GA A#AGE A#AGE F# G A#

BD'G BD'G BD'G BD'G BD'G' D'BG

BD'G BD'G BD'G BD'G BD'G' D'BG

GBD' GBD' EAC EAC G' E'D'CBAG

A#BD'BG F# F DEF#G BA# GGGG BBBB D'D'D'D' G'

DEF#G B DEF#G BA# GGGG GGGG BGED

DF#AF#D c#c DEF#G BA# GGGG GGGG DEF#G G

The Bouncy (She'll be coming round the mountain)

DEGGGGGEDbDG GABBB BD'D'D' BA

D'C BBBAG GGGGCC D' CBBBB AAAAG

2nd verse of Cock O' The North

D'G'D'E'D'G' D'E'D' BBBAGA

D'G'D'E'D'G'D'E'D' BBABAG

The Connaughtman's Rambles

AGF# AA D'AA BAA D'AGF#AA D' F#'E'D' BBB

AF# AAD'AABABD'E'F#'G'F#'E'D' F#'E'D' BBB

E'F#'B'B'F#A'A' F#'E'F#'D'E'G'F#'
B'B'F#'A'A'F#'E'D'E'E'

F#'B'B'F#'A'A'F#'E'F#'D'E'F#'G'F#'E'D'F#'E'D' BBB

Scotch on the Rocks

F#F# GEE F# D DEF# GABB A

F#F# GEE F# D D'BD' D'BD' D'BA G

F#F# GEE F# D DEF# GABB A

F#F# GEE F# D DEF#F# GEE D

BGAB GAB D'C#BA F#GA F#GA C# BA

G EF#G EF#G BAGF#D G F#GA

B GAB GAB D'C# BA F#GA F#GA C# BA

GEF#G EF#G BAGF# DE F#ED

E'CD'E' CD'E' G'F#'E' D' BCD' BCD' F#'E'D' CABC ABC E'D CB G C BCD'

E'CD'E' CD'E' G'F#'E' D' BCD' BCD' F#'E'D' CABC ABC E'D'C BGA BAGG

Ger The Rigger

D'GD'G D'E'D'CBG C BCD'E'F#'G'D'E'D'

D'GD'G D'E'D'CBG C'EC BD' BAGABG

G'D'E'D'BD' G'D'E'D'BD' C BCD'E'F#'G'D'E'D'

G'D'E'D'BD' G'D'E'D'BD' C'EC BD' BAGABG

Walsh's Hornpipe

BAGAB DEGBD' CD'E'A BCD'E'

E'D'BD'G'DB GABCBGAGE

GAB DEGBD' CD'E'A BCD'E'

 E'D'BD'G'DB GABCBAG

D'E'F#'G'D'B'D'E'D'B'D'G'D'B'D'E'D'B

AGABD'E'D'BGABCBGAGE

GAB DEGBD' CD'E'A BCD'E'

E'D'BD'G'D'B GABCBAG

Fifer in the Cregagh Glen

EE BB AGAF#GE AF# DD EF# A F#F#

BEBB AGAF#GE AF#D DF#A GEE

BBE'E' F#'G'F#'E'F#D' E'B AA GABE'E'

BB E'E' F#'G'F#'E'D'B 'E'D' B BAGB E E

G GABAG CD'E'G'D' GCD'E'G'D'BG DE'D'CBA

DG ABAG CD'E'G'D'   GCD'E'G'D'BG E'D' BABG

BBE'E' F#'G'F#'E'F#D' E'B AA GABE'E'

BB E'E' F#'G'F#'E'D'B 'E'D' B BAGB E E

Sir Henry Pottinger

b EEF#G EF# bb Dbb cbb

bEEF#G EF# bb cbagab

b EEF#G EF# bb Dbb Cbb

bEEF#G EF# bb cbaf#ge

Ecbabc EDE bagab abcb agaf#g egb

Ecbabc EDE bagab abc cbag aga f#ge

b EEF#G ABCBAB BCBABAG AGAG EF#

b EEEF# G ABCBAB BCBABAG AGAF#GE

Ecbabc EDE bagab abcb agaf#g egb

Ecbabc EDE bagab abc cbag aga f#ge

Killybawn Braes

D'C# BAB EDE BABC#D'C# B AF#D DED

F#EF#GA

D'C# BAB EDE BABC#D' E'D'C# B AF#D EF#EE

C#D'E'F#' E'E'D'B E'D'E'F# 'G'F#''E' D'F#'D'D' AF#
AD'F#'D'D'

C#D'E'F#' E'E'D'B E'D'E'F# 'G'F#''E' D'C# B AF# D
EF#EE

Drops of Brandy (Polka)

D'E'F#' D'E'C#D' C#BAGF# AD' F# EAA

D'E'F#' D'E'C#D' C#BAGF# AB C# D' DD

F# AAA AG BBB B F# AAAF#E A

AGF# AD'F#'G'E'D' C# D'BAGF#ED

D'E'F#' D'E'C#D' C#BAGF# AD' F# EAA

D'E'F#' D'E'C#D' C#BAGF# AB C# D' DD

The Londonderry Clog

AGF# AD'F#'D'AF#G BD'G'D'BGF# AD'F#'C#AF#E

GBE'C#AG F# AD'F#'D'AF#G BD'G' A'GF#A'F#'D'

C#D'E'C#D'F#'D'

F#'G'A'F#'D'A'D'F#'A'G'E'C#A C#E'G'A'F#'D'AD'

G'F#'E'F#' D'C#D' BA

F#'G'A'F#'D'A'D'F#'A'G'F#'E'F#'G' A'GF#A'F#'D'

C#G'E'C#D'F#'D'

Von Ryan's Express

DF#AD' F#'E'D'BA GF# F#GF#DE
F#AD'F#' G'F#'E'D'A G'F#' A'G'E'D'

AGF#AD#' F#'E'D'BG' BA D'D'E'F#'G'E'
AGF#AD' F#'E'D'BG' BA D'E'E'D'C#D'

DF#AD' F#'E'D'BA GF# F#GF#DE
F#AD'F#' G'F#'E'D'A G'#F' A'G'E'D'

Four Step Volunteers

BBBAAG G'G'F'E' D'BBCD'D' BAAABA

BBBAAG G'G'F'E' D'BBCD'D' GACBAG

BAG G'F'E D'BBCD'BA

BAG G'F'E' D'BBCD'D' GACBAG

China Man's Delight

G A B A G C B A D` C B E` F` G`

D` E` D`D` B C D` C B A

G A B A G C B A D` C B E` F` G`

D` E` D`D` B C D` C F E

D` G` D`D` G`D`D` E` D` C D`

G A B D` E` D`D`E` D` C B A

D` G` D`D` G` D`D` E` D` C D`

G A B A G C B A D` C B E` F` G`

D` E` D`D` B C D` C F E DOUBLE 40

G A B A G E D E D G F G

G A B A G C B C A F D

D` E` D`E`E` D` E` D` C B A

G A B A G E D E D G F G

G A B A G C B A D` C B E` F` G`

D` E` D`D` B C D`C B A

G A B A G C B A D` C B E` F` G`

D` E` D`D` B C D` C F E

Mouldy Old Dough

B D'D' A D'D' B D' G' E' D'C
B D'D' A D'D' B D' G'E' D'C
B A B C D'E'D' CBABCB

B D' GG G B D' CC C E'AAA C E' F#'
D' E' F#'G'G'G' G'F#'E'A ABD'E'E'E' E'E' D'BG

BD'G GBD' BD'G GBD' D' G DRUMS

ABD' ABD' ABD' ABD' D' G DRUMS

DRUMS

REPEAT ALL

B D' GG G B D' CC C E'AAA C E' F#'
D' E' F#'G'G'G' G'F#'E'A ABD'E'E'E' E'E' D'BG

Loyal Crossmore

(AKA Wriggleys)
D'BBCD'D'D'CBD' D'BBCD'D'DCB GE'E'F'G'G'
E'D'D'E'F'G'D' CBD'BGACBFG

D'GGAG CBCD'BG D'CBAGFGAFD
DEGCBCD'BG D'CAFDEDEFG

D'BBCD'D'D'CBD' D'BBCD'D'D'CB GE'E'F'G'G
E'D'D'E'F'G'D' CBDBGACBFG

Paschendale

ABA AD'C'BA F#'E'D' BE'BB
D'A ABAAF# DEF# AGED
GAB BCE'DB GAB E'D'BA
GAB BCE'D'B GAB D'CBA
E'F#'G' F#'E'G'D'B E'F#'G' E'D'G'A
GAB BCE'D'B GAB D'CBA

Belfast Lough

intro
BBABD'E'F'G' E'D'BBAG

BBABGBD'D' E'E'D'E'D'GB BBABGBAG AAGABA
BBABGBD'D' E'E'D'E'D'GB BBABGBAG CBGBAG

D'D'G'G' F#'F#'G'E' G'E'D'D'BA BBABD'E'F#'G'
E'D'BBAG

Bloody Road to the Somme

GBCD' D'E'DBD'G GBCD' D'E'D'BD'
BCD'G'F#'E' D'E'D'D'BD'G GABAG

D'G'F#'E' D'E'D'D'BD'G GG'F#'E' D'E'D'D'BD'
GG'F#'E' D'E'D'D'BD'G GABAG

The Tomb

F#AD'ABAF#A AD'F'D'G'F#'D'F'D'E' E'F#'G'E'F#'D'E'B
D'C'BAD'A G'F#'E'D'A
F#AD'ABAF#A AD'F#'D'G'F#'D'F#'D'E'
E'F#'G'E'F#'D'E'B D'C'BAD'A G'F#'E'D'A ABC'D' AD'

BCD'GGG G'E'D'E'D' CD'GG BCBA BCD'GGG
G'E'D'E'D CBCD' GAGF#G
REPEAT

DRUM SOLO

F#AD'ABAF#A AD'F#'D'G'F#'D'F#'D'E'
E'F#'G'E'F#'D'E'B D'C'BAD'A G'F#'E'D'A
F#AD'ABAFA AD'F#'D'G'F#'D'F'D'E' E'F#'G'E'F#'D'E'B
D'C'BAD'A G'F#'E'D'A ABCD'.......AD' D'

Cumbernauld

D'E'F#'F#'G'F#'E'D'BD'D'E'D D'E'F#'F#'G'F#'E'D'E'
D'E'F#'F#'G'F#'E'D'BD'D'E'D' D'E'F#'F#'E'E'F#'E'D'

ABC'D'E' F#'G'F#'E'D'C'D'BD'E'D'E'F#'F#
F#'G'F#'D'E' F#'G'F#'E'D'C'D'E'BC'D'E'
ABC'D'E' F#'G'F'E'D'C'D'BD'E'D'E'F#'F#'
F#'G'F#'D'E' F#'G'F#'E'D'C'D'E'E'F#'E'D'

Killiecrankie

D'E'F#'F#'F#'E'D'G'G'G' G'F#' F#'G'F#'E'D'F#'E'E'
D'E'F#'F#'F#'E'D'G'G'G' G'F#'F#'G'A'F#'E'D'B D'D'

D'E'F#'AA D'C'BD' GG G'F#' F#'G'F#'E'D'F#'E'E'
D'E'F#'AA D'C'BD' GG G'F#'F#'G'A'F#'E'D'B D'D'

D'E'F#'F#'F#'E'D'G'G'G' G'F#' F#'G'F#'E'D'F#'E'E'
D'E'F#'F#'F#'E'D'G'G'G' G'F#'F#'G'A'F#'E'D'B D'D'

Hunters Purse

E'F#'G'F#'G' E'F#'G' G'F#'G'E'D' CBCD'E'
E'D'CD'E'F#'G'E'D'
E'F#'G'F'G' E'F#'G' G'F#'G'E'D' CBCD'E' E'D'CA BAGA

E'AAGAGE F#G GF#GEE CBCD'E' E'D'CD'E'F#'G'E'D'
E'AAGAGE F#G GF#GEE CBCD'E' E'D'CA BAGA

E'F#'G'F'G' E'F#'G' G'F#'G'E'D' CBCD'E'
E'D'CD'E'F#'G'E'D'
E'F#'G'F'G' E'F#'G' G'F#'G'E'D' CBCD'E' E'D'CA BAGA

The Pipers Call

Intro F#'G'G'F#' D'E'E'D CBG BAG

 AF#AAD'BA AGFA D'D'E' D'E'F#'F#'E' C'D'BA
GF#F#GFE
AF#AAD'BA AGF#A D'D'E' D'E'F#'F#'E C'D'BA
GF#DF#ED

D'BD'D'E'D' CBD' G'F#'E' F#'G'G'F#' D'E'E'D' CBBCBA
D'BD'D'E'D' CBD' G'F#'E' F#'G'G'F#' D'E'E'D' CBG BAG
DRUMS

D'BD'D'G'E'D' CBD' G'G'A' GABBA F#'G'E'D' CBBCBA
D'BD'D'G'E'D' CBD' G'G'A' GABBA F#'G'E'D' CBG BAG

D'BD'D'E'D' CBD' G'F#'E' F#'G'G'F#' D'E'E'D' CBBCBA
D'BD'D'E'D' CBD' G'F#'E' F#'G'G'F#' D'E'E'D' CBG BAG

Old Holborne

EAEABCBAEAEABC DGDGABAGDGDGAB
EAEABCBAEAEABC BCBCE'D'B CBAGBA

EAEAE EABC BCE'D'B CBAGAE
EAEAE EABC BCE'D'B CBAGA
CD'E'E' E'D'BD'E'D' D'E'D'B B G'F#'G'F#'E'
EAEAE EABC BCE'D'B CBAGA

The Twelfth

AGF# AD' GBD' G'F#' D'C#D'E' C#D'

AGF# AD' GBD' G'F#' D'C#D'E 'D'C#BA

AGF# AD' GBD' G'F#' D'C#D'E'C#D'

G'F#'D'F#'A'F#'D'E' G'F#'D'F#'A' F#'E'D'BA

A'G'F#'A' D' GBD' G'F#'D'C#D'E'C#D'

AGF# AD' GBD' G'F#' D'C#D'E'D'C#BA

AGF# AD' GBD' G'F#' D'C#D'E'C#D'

DGGG BD'BG BD'BG D AAA GF#AD

DGGG BD'BG BD'BG DAAA DGBG

D'CB GG D'CB GG E'D'C#AA C#D'E'AA

C#D'E'AD'AE'AD' AGF#A DF#G

Titoli

EA BCD' CBAG EGA EA BCD' CBAG EGE

EA BCD' CBABCD'E' G'E'E'C G'E'E'C AD' ABC AGA

EA BCD' CBAGEGA EABCD' CBAGEGE

EAC E'D'CD'E' F'E'D'CC D' AGAA

E ABA EABA EABCBAGEGABAGE

E ABA EABA GCD'E'D'CBG BCBC CBAGA D'
BCBAGA

EA BCD' CBAG EGE GCD'E'F'E'D'C D'CBA

C E' G' E'E'E'C CE' A' E'E'E' C AD' ABC AGA

E ABA EABA EABCBAGEGABAGE

E ABA EABA GCD'E'D'CBG BCBC CBAGA D'
BCBAGA

BE' F#'G'F#'E'D' E' B F#'F#' G'F#'E'D'E'

BE' F#'G'F#'E'D' E' B F#'F#' G'F#'E'D'E'

The Toreador Song

GAGE EEDEFE FD GE cadg

d AGFEDEFE Beed# f B

BAG# A EF#G ED BA Da GF#ED

       D E F#

GAGE EEDEFE FD GE cadg

d AGFEDEFE Beed# f B

BAG# A EF#G ED BA Da GF#ED

The Gambler

BAG GAGGD GB D'D'E'E'D' G

D'E'E'D' G GF#GA

BAG GAGGD GB D'D'E'E'D'G

D'E'E'D'B G ACBAG

The Coward of the County

AAA BAGF# ABB D' B F#A BAAA BAGF# F#G F#EDE

AAABAGF# ABB D' BF#A AABBAF# DEGF#ED

ABC#D' C#D'E'D' BF#A D'D'D'C# BA GF#E

AB C#D' D'C#D' E'D' BF#A AAABAGF#E A F#G AAA
BAGEc#D

Merrymen

dgabbab GBDD EF#GF#EED b bb aaa

bgabbab gbD D EF#GF#EEDbbb gg

dgabbab GBDD EF#GF#EED b bb aaa

bgabbab gbD D EF#GF#EEDbbb gg

DGF#G EF#GABG#G F#D EGF#EDb bb aaa

bgabbab gbD D EF#GF#EEDbDb gg

DGF#G EF#GABG#G F#D EGF#EDb bb aaa

bgabbab gbD D EF#GF#EEDbDb gg

Malbrouk

GA BBBABCB CBAAAGABG

GABBBABC C D'BGABG

BCD'D'E'E'D' BCD'D'E'E'D'

One More Bottle

DGB D'D'BG CE'E'E' D'CB D'G'D'BG AF# DDD

D GF# GEF#G ABCD'E'F#'G'

F#'E'D'F#'G'A'G'F#'E'D'CB GGG

BD'BAF#DDD F#GABCD'E'F#'G'

F#'E'D' G'F#'G'A'G'F#'E'D' CB GGG

D GGG ABCD' B GC D'CBGG

GE'E'E' BD' BABAG GB D'E'D G C BA AAG

Johnny Gone Down to Hilo

G E'E'E'E'D'D'E'E'D' D'E'D'

BAG BGED GGG BD'E'D' BAG

G'E'D' G'F#'E'D' G'F#'E'D' BAG BGED

GGG BD'E'D' BAG

One more day

 ABAF#ED ABA D' CBAG BCD' BAG

F#G AABBA F#ED ABA D'CBAG BCD' BA*G

Sweet Ladies of Plymouth

DGGABAG CD'E'D' D'E' D'CBA

DGG ABAG CD'E'D' D'C BAGAGF#G

ABCD'E'D' CBA D'CBAG AGF#G

No Hopers, Jokers & Rogues

D D'D'D' CBAG B D DD EGG BBBCBA

BB BBCBAGE GD D D'D'D'D' CBA BAG

D D'D'D' CBAG B D DD EGG BBBCBA

D'D'D' CBAG AB D DEEF# F#GGA BCB AGG BA

D D'D'D' CBAG B D DD EGG BBBCBA

BB BBCBAGE GD D D'D'D'D' CBA BAG

D AA GF# GF#EEDD D AA GF# GF#EEDD

 DE EF# AG GA ABAA

D D'D'D' CBAG B D DD EGG BBBCBA

BB BBCBAGE GD D D'D'D'D' CBA BA*G

Carson of the UVF

DEF#GG AF#G DGGAF#G DGGGGAEF#

F#AA B F#A F#AABF#A F#D'CBAB

CD'E' GCE'E'D'D'CD' D'D'D' EG CCBBAB

DEF#GGAF#G ABBCAB BCD'F#'E'D'C BF#G

Rakes of Kildare

EbEEF#EF# GGAB C#D'C#D' BD' BAGF#E

Eb EEF#EF#GGAB C#D'C# BAGF#E E

E'E'B E'E'B E'D'C#D' B C#D'C#D' BD' BAGF#E

E'E'B E'E'B E'D'C#D'B C#D'C# BAGF#EE

Castles in The Air

DEF#GG BD DEF#GF#GAB BC BCE'D'BAGABAGE

DEF#GG BD DEF#GF#GAB BC BCE'D' BGABCBAG

D'E'EG'D'D' BCBCD'B C BCE'D'BAGABAGE

DEF#GG BD DEF#GF#GAB BC BCE'D' BGABCBAG

Atholl Highlanders

BCD'D' BG D'BG ABC D'D'BG ABCBAG

D'D'BG D'BGABC D'G'D'E'D' CBCAG

D'GBD' GBD' GCE' GCE' GBD' GBD' ABCB A

GBD' GBD' GCE' GCE' D'G'D'E'D' CBCAG

D'G' D'D'D' CB G'D'D'D'CB G'D' D'D'C BABCBAG

G' D'D'D' CB G'D'D'D'CB G'D'D'D'E'D' CBCAG

G A BG BBG BCA CCA CBG BBG BAF# AAF#

ABG BBG BCA CCA CD'G'D'E'D' CBCAG

Spirit of Ulster

BAAG EAA AABAAG EAABA F#G F#AG DGG GG
DGGABAGF#G

DGAB BA BAG GE'E'D'CBA BBAGGE' E'E'D'D'C
GABCBABAGE' GABCBA BAG

The Entertainer

EFF#D'F#D'F#D' D'E'F'F#' D'E'F#' C#E'D'

EFF#D'F#D'F#D' C# BAG# BD'F#' E'D'BE'

EFF#D'F#D'F#D' D'E'F'F#' D'E'F#' C#E'D'

D'E'F#' DE'F#' D'E'D' F#' D'E'F#' D'E'D' F#' D'E'F#'

C#E'D'

FGG# ABA FGG#ABA F#'E'D' ABD'E'F#'E'D'E'D'

FGG# ABA FGG#ABA ABC# E'E'E' C#BAD'

FGG# ABA FGG#ABA F#'E'D' ABD'E'F#'E'D'E'D'

D'BD'C#BAG# BD'E'F#' E'D' BAD'F#'E'D'

Cockleshell Bay

A F#'G'F#' D'E'F#'E' C# D'E'D' C# BA BC#D' BC#D'E'

D' F#'G'F#'E'

A F#'G'F#' D'E'F#'E' C# D'E'D' C# BA BC#D' BC#D'E'

C#D' C#D'

BD' BA D' GAG F#ED BD' BA D' E'F#'G'F#'E'

A F#'G'F#' D'E'F#'E' C# D'E'D' C# BA BC#D' BC#D'E'

C#D' C#D'

Hearts of Glory

BCD'E'D' GGABD BBBCD'E'D' D'D'E'F#'G'

G'G'G' F#' E'E'D' BBCD'E' GB GC BA G

BCD'E'D' GGABD BBBCD'E'D' D'D'E'F#'G'

G'G'G' F#' E'E'D' BBCD'E' GB GC BAGF#G

D'BD'E'D' BCD'E' D'BD'E'D' D'E'F#'G'

G'F#'E'E'D' E'E'D' BBCD'E' GB GC BA G

Williamites

DD AA BC AA BCAA GA BCBA

AD AA BCAB CBAA GABCB A

AD'F#'E' E'F#'G'E'F#' F#'E'E' E'F#'G'E'F#'

AD'F#'E' E'F#'G'E'F#' F#'E'E' D'E'F#'E'D'

BBABAF# ABABC#D' BBABAF# EF#AB

D'D'C#D' E'F#' E'D' C# E'D'BA F#'F#' BBA F#EF#AB

BD'E' F#'F#' BBA F#EF#AB

D'D'C#D' E'F#' E'D' C# E'D' F#'E'

BBABAF# EF#AB

D'D'C#D' E'F#' E'D' C# E'D'BA F#'F#' BBA F#EF#AB

BD'E' F#'F#' BBA F#EF#AB

John Condon

D D'D' DD D'C D' B CBAGE EE E'E' EE D'D' GABC
BAG EF#

GG GABE F#GG ABCD' G'F#'E' DE'G'B AB AGG

The Final Trawl

GABBB AGABG BD'E'G'E'D' BD'E'B

BABD'B AGABG EGABA GEGAD

GABBB AGABG BD'E'G'E'D' BD'E'B

BABD'B AGABG EGABA GEGAD

1941

AABAGF#A DDDEF# AF#'G'F#'E'D'E'D'BA BAGF#
AABAGF#A DDDEF# AF#'G'F#'E'D'E'D'BA D'C#'D'

D'C#'D' D'C#D' D'C#D'F#'A D'C#D' D'C#D'F#'A
D'C#D' D'C#D' D'C#D'F#'A G'F#'E'D'

AABAGF#A D'D'D'E'F#' AF#'G'F#'E'D'E'D'BA BAGF#
AABAGF#A D'D'D'E'F#' AF#'G'F#'E'D'E'D'BA G'F#'E'D'
D'

McAlpine's Fusiliers

E'F#'G'F#'E' D'BAGE GABBG F#G

D'D'BD' E'F#'G'F#'E' D'E'F#'E'D'BABD'E'

D'D'BD' E'F#'G'F#'E' D'E'F#'E'D'BABD'E'

E'F#'G'F#'E' D'BAGE GABBG F#G

Prisoner's Letter

D'D'D'CBAG ABCD'E'D' BD'G'D'CBG BD'CBCA

D'D'D'CBAG ABCE'G'D' BD'G'D'CBG BD'CE'F#'G'

Flower of Ulster

AF#'E'F#'G'F#'D' C#BGBD'A AF#'A'G'F#'F#'E'E'

F#'E'D'C#BA

AF#'E'F#'G'F#'D' C#BGBD'A F#'G'A'A'G'F#'F#'E'B

E'F#'G'E'C#BC#D'

Braveheart

F#AB D'C#D'C#BAA BF# F#AB D'C#D'C#BAB

F#AB F#E DEGF#EDb F#AB D'C#D'C#BAB

BD'E' G'F#'G'F#'E'D'D' E'B BD'E' G'F#'G'F#'E'D'E'

BD'E' BA GACBAGE BD'E' G'F#'G'F#'E'D'E'

Northern Lights of Aberdeen

D'GAGB BA GAG D'E'E'CD'E'D' D'E'CCD' E'D'BAGA ABAGD'

D'GAGB BA GAG D'E'E'CD'E'D' D'E'C G'F#'E'D'BG' G'F#'D'F#' G'G'

D'D'BCD' D'G'F'E'D' BD'CBAD' D'D'BCD' D'G'F#'E'D' BD'CBAG

D'E'C E'G'F#' E'F#'D'B D'E'C E'G'F#' E'F#' D'D'B'CD' D'G'F#'E'D' BD'CBAG

D'G GB BA GAG D'E'E'CD'E'D' D'E'CCD' E'D'BAGA ABAGD'

D'G GB BA GAG D'E'E'CD'E'D' D'E'C G'F#'E'D'BG' G'F#'D'#F' G'G'

Painted Clouds

DG BD'D'D' D'E'CBBB D'CBAD AD D'CB

DGB D'D'D' D'E'C BBB D'CBA D AD AG

DGDGB GB D'C#D'E'D'B CBCD'CA

D'C#D'E'D'B DG DGB GBD'C#D'E'D'B

CBCD'CA CBAG

BCD'E CE'E'E'D B

BD'D'D'C#D'E'D'C#BA GF#ED

DG DGB GBD'C#D'E'D'B

CBCD'CA CBAG

Running Bear

ABF#A ABAD'F#' F#'E'D'B BC#D'A

ABF#A ABAD'F#' D'D'D' B BC#D'E'

ABF#A ABAD'F#' F#'E'D'B BC#D'A

ABF#A ABAD'F#' AAA F#'E'C#D'

D'D'D'D' B D'E'D' BA AAABAGF#

D'D'D'D' B D'E'D' BA AAA F#'E'C#D'

Littlest Hobo

BAG GBBBAGA BAG GE'E'E'CD'

E'F#'G'G'G' G'G'F#'F#'E'

E'E'D'E' E'E'D'E' D'D' BAG

G'G'F#'F#'E' E'E'E'D'E'B

BBD' BA ABCCBAG

D'E'F#'G'G'G'G'F#'F#'E'

E'E'D'E' E'E'D'E' D'D' BAG

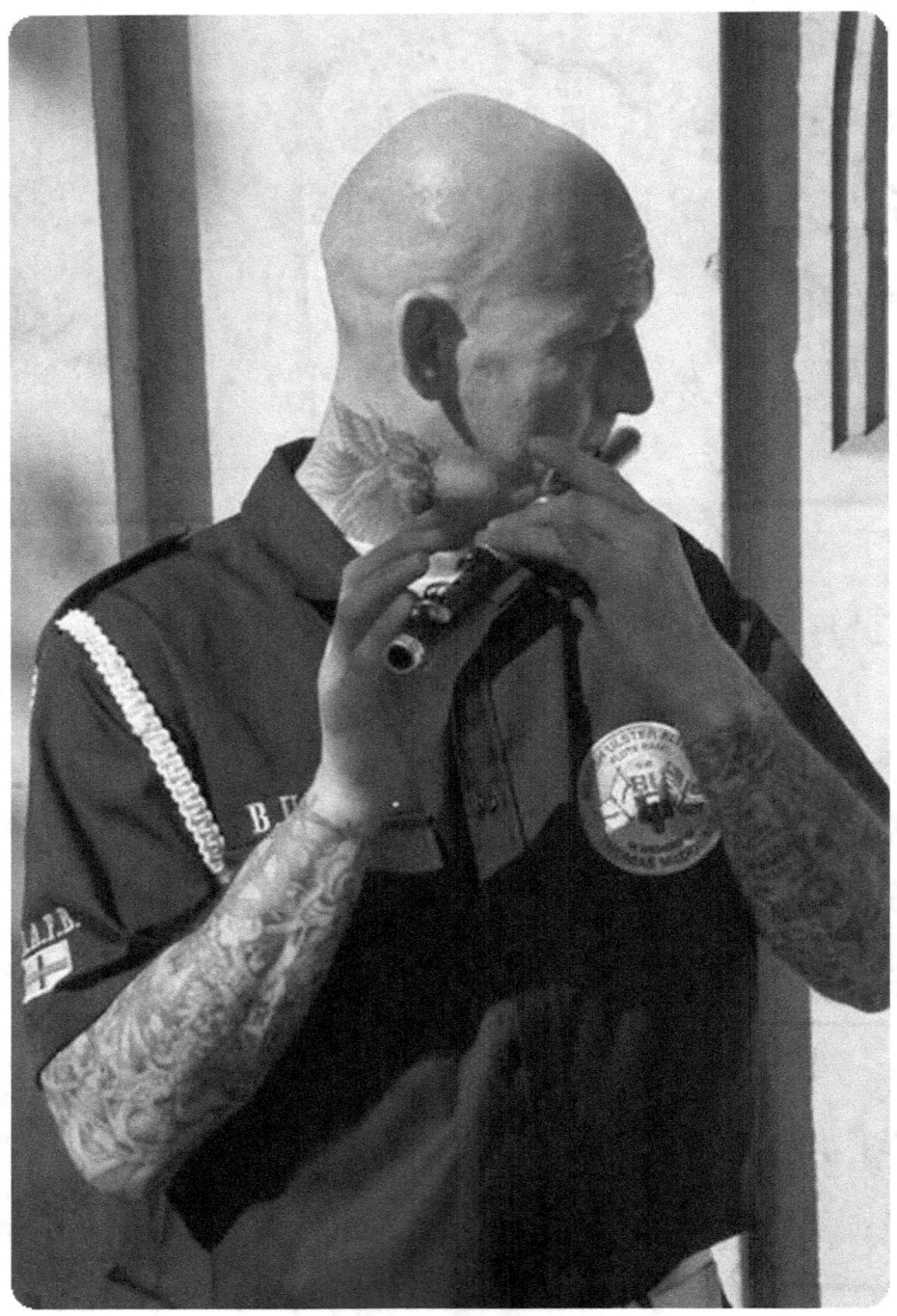

Above, A Fluter from the British Ulster Alliance Flute Band - England

Gusty's Jig

GAB CBAB EF#GABAG F#GF#ED

BCB AB EF#G ABAGF#E

BCD'E' D'E' BD'E'F#'G'F#'E'D'E'D'B CD'E'
D'E'BD'E'F#'G'F'E'D'B /Repeat

E'B .. E'B.. E'BAGAB..

GABCB E'BAG ABC F#GE../Repeat

E'D'C B CBAB EF#GABAG F#GF#ED

BCB AB EF#G ABAGF#E

BCD'E' D'E' BD'E'F#'G'F#'E'D'E'D'B CD'E'
D'E'BD'E'F#'G'F'E'D'B

E'B..E'B..E'BAGAB..

GABCB E'BAG ABC F#GE../Repeat

E'B E'B E'B …

Ghostriders in the Sky

EEE F# GGG EDDD bD

DEEE F#GGG ABB CBAGB D'B

A# B E'E'D'E'B A# B A# B GE ccc EGGG GG AF# DE

BBB D' E'E'D'E'D'B GE cccEGGG GG AF# DE

BBBD' E'E'D'E'D'B GE cccEGGG GG AF# DE

Battlefields

DEG G'B AGABAGA DEG G'BD'E'

DEG G'B AGABAGA DEG G'BAG

BCD' G'F'G' BCD'E'D' BCD' G'F'G' BD'

BCD' G'F'G' BCD'E'D' BAG G' BAG

A Touch of Heather

GGGABGABA BAGGGABCD'E'D'

D'E'F'G'E'D' D'E'D'CBA BAG G'D'E'D'CBG

(repeat)

G'G' GABGABA BGG'G' GABCD'E'D'

D'E'F'G'E'D' D'E'D'CBA BAG G'D'E'D'CBG

(repeat)

GFGDEFGD BCD'BABA GFGDEFGD BCD'BAG

BCD'BCBAD BCD'BA BCD'BCBA DEFGD E F

GGGABGABA BAGGGABCD'E'D'

D'E'F'G'E'D' D'E'D'CBA BAG G'D'E'D'CBG

G'G' GABGABA BGG'G' GABCD'E'D'

D'E'F'G'E'D' D'E'D'CBA BAG G'D'E'D'CBG

4th of July

G'E'CCC AGBD'BC AGC AGC AGB

AGBCD' BCD'E' CD'E' CD'E' CD'

G'E'CCC AGBD'BC CBABCG E'D'

GCBC E'D'C'D' GAC BCD'C

BCD'BGABCD' G'E'C F'F'E'D'E'F'D'B

BCD'BGABCD' G'E'C F'F'E'D'E'F'D'G'

Peoples Army

BCD' BCD' G'F'E' CBA G'F'F'F' E'F'F'F' E'D'D'E'CB

BCD' BCD' G'F'E' CBA G'F'F'F' E'F'F'F' E'D'D'E'F'G'

(repeat) (G' AFTER REPEAT)

D'BCD'G' G'E'CD'E' E'F'F'E'D' E'F'G'G'E'D'

D'BCD'G' G'E'CD'E' E'F'F'E'D' E'F'G'G'F'G'

Black Hawk Down

A F# D D E G F# E D F E F# A D`

D` E` F#` F#` E` E` D` D` B A A B A G F#

A F# D D E G F# E D F# E F# A D`

D` E` F#` F#` E` E` D` B A B D` E` D`

D` C` C` B A F# A B A F# A

D` D` C# C# B A F# A B A F# E

F# E D D E G F# E D F# E F# A D`

D` E` F#` F#` E` E` D` B A B D` E` D`

Far off fields of Picardy

BCD'BAG ABAGE BCD'BAG ABAGA

BCD'BAG ABAGE DGGGABBAFG

E'E'D'CD'B GEE'D'CD' E'E'D'CD'BAGABAGE

D'E'E'D'CD'B GE'E'D'CD' GGGABBAFG

BBBABCD'B CCCBCABCD' E'E'F'G'F'G'E'D'B
AAABCCBAG

Maintain the Union

E ABCBAGA E E A BCBCF'E'

E'F' F'E'D'E'A EA BCBAGA

E'F' F'E'D'E'A EA BCBAGA

F'A' A'G'F'E'A ABC E'DCE'

F'A' A'G'F'E'A ABC E' BCA

Hearts of Oak

A D'D'D'D' F#'E'D' C# BA ABB C#D' E'F#'G' F#'E'F#'

F#'E'D'F# BA F#'E'D'F#BA A F#'E'D' A' C#D'E'E'E'A

E'E'E'C#D'E' F#'F#'F#'D'E'F#' F#'E'D'C# F#'D'B

C#AF#D F# AB C#D'E' F#' E'D' A' C#D'

The Promise

GAB BCBAG GGABBCBA

CC CD' CBAA D'D'E'D'CB

BCD'D'E'D'CBB D'D'D'ED'C

D'E'D'E'G'E'D' ABCD'BAG

Admiral Benbow's Reel

DGAGF#GAGED GbDG DGAGF#G BAG E'D'BA

DGAGF#GAGED GbDG GABD'E'D'BG ABAGF#G

GCE'GCE' GBD'GBD' BD' BAGAB E'D'BA

GCE'GCE' GBD'GBD' GABD'E'D'BG ABAGF#G

Shanendoah

GB D'E'D G C BAA G

D GGG ABCD' B GC D'CBGG

GE'E'E' BD' BABAG GB D'E'D G C BA AA G

Bonnie Doon

DG GA GABD' BA GABAGGE DDEGA

BAG GA GABD'BA GABAGGE DDEGG

BD'E'D'BG D'E'D'BG D'BG D'BG E'D'CBA

BAG GA GABD'BA GABAGGE DDEGG

The Campbells Are Coming

D F#ABAF#D F#F#F# DF#ABAF#DEEE

DF#ABAF#D ABC#D' E'F#' D'BD' AF#D EEE

AD'D'D'E'F#'AAA AD'D'D'E'F#' BBB

AAB C#D'C# BABC#D' E'F#' D'BD' AF#D EEE

The Fallen Hero

BAG EDbD DEG CBAGA

BAG EDbD DEG CBBAG

BD'D'E'D'BD' BD'D'E'E'D'BGA

BD'D'E'D'BD' D CBAG BAG

BD'D'E'D'BD' BD'D'E'E'D'BGA

BAG EDbD DEG CBBAG

Dainty Davie

DD GABCD'E'D'C CB CBAGG bc#D

D GABCD'E'D'C D'CB AGABCB A G

D'E'CA BCD'BG ABC BAG F#GAF#D

EF#GABCD'E'DC CBAGABC BA G

In Flanders Fields

GCD'E' D'CAA AD'E'F' E'D'CB

G E'F'G' F'E'D'C A F'E'D'CB

           ABC

GCD'E' D'CAA AD'E'F' E'D'CB

G E'F'G' F'E'D'C D'D'

GCD'E' DCAA AD'E'F' E'D'CB

G E'F'G' F'E'D'C A F'E'D'CB

ABC ABC ABC

DGAB AGEE EABC BAGF#

DBCD' CBAG E CBAGF# EF#G

The Big Country

AGF#A D'C#D'E'F#'D' AGF#A D'C#D'F#'E'

AGF#A D'C#D'E'F#'D'BA D'E'F#'D' BAD'E'D'

Hail to the Chief

A BA F#'E'D' BGB D'C#BA BAA D' E'F#' E'D'E'

A BA F#'E'D' BGB D'C#BA BAA D'F#'E'C#E'D'

F#'D'F#'A'F#'D'E' F#'E'E'C#A

F#'D'F#'A'F#'D' B E'E'E'

F#'D'F#' A'F#'D' BGB D'C#B

ABAA D'F#'E'C#E'D'

BAF#D BAF#D DF# A A' G'F#' E'F#'E'D'

DF# A A' G'F#' E'F#'E'D'

Glenlogie

BBB ABBABBAF#

D'E'F#'F#' E'D'D'B D'BAF#AB

D'E'F#'F#' E'D'E'E' F#'E'D'B AF#E

D'C#BADEDEF# D'C#B

Battle of Somme Eve

DGGF#GAAGABG GE'E'E'F#'G'G'F#'E'D'

GE'E'E'F#'G'G'F#'E'D'G GABD'BGDF#ABG

GE'E'E'F'G'G'F'E'D'B GE'E'E'F'G'G'F'E'D'

GE'E'E'F'G'G' E'D'D'D'E'BG GABD'BGDFABG

3rd Battalion

AF#GAD' A F#GA AF#GA F#'F#'E'D'F#'E'

E'F#'E'D'E' E'F#'E'D' F#'F#' AAA F#'E'D'

Drums

AF#GAD' A F#GA AF#GA F#'F#'E'D'F#'E'

E'F#'E'D'E' E'F#'E'D' F#'F#' AAA F#'E'D'

AF#GAD' A F#GA AF#GA F#'F#'E'D'F#'E'

E'F#'E'D'E' E'F#'E'D' F#'F#' AAA F#'E'

F#' AAAA F#'E' F#' AAAF#'E' D'

Doc Boyd

GCBCGEGCE'A'G' E'F'A'F'A D'BD'BG

AB GCBCGEGCE'A'G' EF'D' BGABCCC

GAAA GF# GGG EF'F'F' E'D' G'E'C

GAAA GF# GGG EF'D' BGABCCC

Away Away

D'E'F#'G'F#'G'E'D' CB E' CAE AGF# D'C#D'E'D'CAB

D'E'F#'G'F#'G'E'D' CB E'CAE AGF# D'C#D'E'D'CAG

BAGF#EF# AC AAGGAB GF#GABCD'E'DD'A

D'E'F#'G'F#'G'E'D' CB E'CAE AGF# D'C#D'E'D'CAB

D'E'F#'G'F#'G'E'D' CB E'CAE AGF# D'C#D'E'D'CAG

Corned Beef Hash

BCD'D'CBA D'D'D'CBA D'D'D' CBAG

D'C BBG A BABG DEF# D'D'D' CBA

GF#G A F#GA F#G AABC BAG GGF#GABAB

D'C BBG A BABG DEF# D'D'D' CBA

GF#G A F#GA F#G AABC

BCD'D'CBA D'D'D'CBA D'D'D' CBAG

GF#GAAA D' CCBAB GF#ED AAAD' CCBAB

GGBD' D' CBAGF#EDE E'D'BGD

E'D'E'D'GD E'D'BGD BAG

Noel Kinner

GAB BA AB G'F#'E' D'B GA F#G

D'E' D'E' G' BAG BD'G'G'BA

D'E' D'E' G' BAG BD'G'G'BA

GAB BA AB G'F#'E' D'B GA F#G

Squeak Seymour

GAB BA GEABG EDEGAG

BCD'D'B CD'E'D'CD' BG ABAGE

BCD'D'B CD'E'D'CD' BG ABAGE

GAB BA GEABG EDEGAG

Earl Bley's Jig

A Dc#D EF#G AF# D GF#GE F#GAG E c#DDD

F#GAGE c#DDD

BGDG BAF#D F# A GEc#ac#E DF#GA F#D

BGDG BAF#D C#BAC#E#AC#E D

Westminster

F#GAF#A D'BGB D'AF#AD'F#'

E'D'C#D'E'F#'G' D'E'D'C#BA

F#GAF#A D'BGB D'AF#AD'F#'

E'D'C#D'E'F#'G' C#E'D' D'

... BC#D'C#D'E'F#'D'BA

D'C#D'E'F#'D'BA

F#AD' G#BD' E'D'# BA

F#GAF#A D'BGB D'AF#AD'F#'

E'D'C#D'E'F#'G' C#E'D' D'

DRUMS

E ABC A EE F#GABC D'BG

BABC AEE F'E'D'CBA

B CCC E'D'D'D' E'CCC E'D'BG

BCCC E'D'D'D' F'E'D'CBA

E ABC A EE F#GABC D'BG

BABC AEE F'E'D'CBA

DRUMS

DEF# AF# AEF#D AA

GF#E DEF#GF#EDb BB

GABD' E'F#' E'D'C# BAF#AD'

DEF#EF#AGF#EDb BB

A'D' E'D'#F#'D'F#G'F#'E'D'

E'D'E'F#'G'F'E'D' B E'E'

D'C# BABD' F#'E'D' C# BAF# B D'

D'E'F#'E'D'C# BAGE BBB

Gold In Every Pocket

AD'E'D' BC#D' BAF#D EF#AF#F#ED EF#AA

AD'E'D' BC#D' BAF#D EF#AF#ED ED

AF#' D'EF#'G' A'F#'D' E'F#'D'F#' F#'D'F#' E'D'AA

AF#' D'EF#'G' A'F#'D' E'F#'D'F#' E'F#'E'D'

Father O'Flynn

AD'AF# DF#A D'E'D'C#BAD'C#D'

E'F#'G'F#'E'F#'

E'C# AD'AF# DF#A D'E'D'C#BAD'C#D' E'F#'G'F#'D'D'

E'F#'D'F#' F#'G'A' E'F#'E' E'C#A

D'C#D' BE'D'C#AA ABGB BC#D' AF#DD

F#A D'C#D' E'F#'G'F#'D'D'

Morning Star Reel

GABABGE F#GABAF#D GABAB GEF#GF#EDGG

GABABGE F#GABAF#D GABAB GEF#GF#EDGG

GABABD'E'F#'G'E'D'E'D'BA

GABABD'E'F#'G'E'F#'D'D'

D'ABAB D'E'F#'G'E'D'E'D'BA

GABABGEF#GF#E DGG

Young Men in their Bloom

EGE GEG BGB E' E'F#'G'F#''E' D'C# BABGF#ED

EGE GEG BGB E' E'F#'G'F#''E' D'C# BAGF#E

EGE BB EGE BC#D' DED AA F#DF# AGF#

EGE BB EGE E' E'F#'G'F#''E' D'C# BAGF#E

The Grand Spy

DEF#F# AGF#ED F#AA ABABC#D' C#BABC#D'

F#F# AGF#ED F#AA ABABC#D' AF#EE

E B E'E' D'E'F#'G'F#'G'E' BC#D'F#'D'D'AF#AD'F#'D'D'

C# B E'E' D'E'F#'G'F#'G'E'

D'C#BABC#D'A F#EE

The Tenpenny Bit

D'C#BE BE F#EF# DF#A BE BE ABD'E'F#'E'

BE BE F#EF# DF#A BABD'AF# F#EDE

B E'E'D'E' F#'E'F#' D'BA B E'E'D'E' F#'E'F#' D'

D'B E'E'D'E' F#'E'F#' D'BA ABC# D'AF# F#EDE

Sapper Hill

EEA BCBA CBAG BA E

EEA BCBA CBAG BA

E'E'D'E'D'C D'E'F'E'D'EA

E'E'D'E'D'C D'E' A'A'G'A'

E'E'D'E'D'C D'E'F'E'D'EA

E'E'D'E'D'C D'E' AAGA

E AA GA GEDE ABC CCBACB GED

E AA GA GEDE ABC C D'C BCB GA

EEA BCBA CBAG BA E

EEA BCBA CBAG BA

A Proud History

F#GA AA D'BD' A GF#GF#ED

AD'D'D' E'F#'G'G'F#' G'F#'E'D'BA

A D'D'D' E'F#'G'G'F#' G'F#'E'D' BA

F#GAAA D'BD' A GF#GF#ED

Olde Southern Medley

BCD' BC AB GA …

BCD' BCAB GA BCD' BCAB GA BCD' BCAB GA
DGGABGBA DGGAB . GF#

GCCE'E'DE'D BA BAGG DEG CE'DBAGABG G

BCD' BC AB GA …

BCD' BCAB GA BCD' BCAB GA BCD' BCAB GA

BAGF#GAG bcDEDbD GABBBAGABAA

BAGF#GAG bcDEDbD GABD'E' BAGABAG

BD'BD'D' BD'BD'D' CE'CE'E' CE'CE'E'
G'G'D'D'BD'BAG GABD'E'D'BGA BAG

BD'BD'D' BD'BD'D' CE'CE'E' CE'CE'E'
G'G'D'D'BD'BAG GABD'E'D'BGA BD' G'

Two Little Boys

F#'E'D'E'F#'D'D'BA F#'E'D'E'F#' B G'F#'E'G'
D'E'F#'E'D'B C#D' F#'E'D'C# BE'

F#'E'D'E'F#'D'D'BA F#'E'D'E'F' B G'F#'E'G'
D'E'F#'E'D'B C#D' E'E'E'E'E' A

F#G A BAA D'E'F#'E'D' D'E'F#'E'D'E'F#' B G'F#'G' F#'
D'E'F#' E' B C#D'F#'E'D'C# B E'

F#G A BAA D'E'F#'E'D' D'E'F#'E'D'E'F#' B BD'
G'G'E'F#'G'F#' B F#'A'F#'E'F#'E'D'

The Polecat

BAG EGDGEG BAGEG E DEF#G

BAGEGDGEG BAGEG ED GF#G

D'BD' G'F#'E'D'E'F# BAG D'B'D'G'F#'E'D'CBA

D'BD' G'F#'E'D'E'F# BAG BAGEG ED GF#G

The Guns of Navarone

DG ABAG E'E'D'BG E'ED'BG D'E'D'CBA

DG ABAG E'E'D'BG E'ED'BG D'E'D'CBA ABBAG

D'D'E'F#'E'D' G'G'F#'E'D' G'G'F#'E'D' E'

D'D'E'F#'E'D' G'G'F#'E'D' E'E'F#'E'D'BD'

Imagine

AA F#A C#C# B AAF#A C# B

AAF#A C#C# B AAF#A C#B

D'D'BD' F#'F#'E' C#C#C#D'E' F# A'F#'E'D'

C#D' C# D'C#B BC#D'D' D'D'C#D'BC#A

C#D' C# D'C#B BC#D'D' C#D'E'D#'E'D'E'F#'D'D'

Family Guy

D'C#D' BC#CC# ACBCBCD' CBBA# B

 EF#GAAG A# G BBCB A# BE'BGED'

D#' E' D#'E'F#'G'F#'E'D' CBCBCD' CB A# B A# BC
BA G# A G# AB F# GG BE' D' D#' E' F#'

A# BCC# D'E'F#'G' G'

The Sleeping Warrior

DGB D' E CB DGB D' CB A GA

DGB D'E GD Gc DED CBB ABAG

EGc DED Gb DGB D' CBAG F#E D

DGB D'E GD Gc DED CBB ABAG

F#G D CB ABAG

Ulster Girl

AGF#A D' AABB BA E'D'C#BA

F#F# AA ABC#D' F#E BBAG#A

A G'G'G' G' F#'E'E' AF#'F#'E'F#'D'

BB C#D' BA D'D' D'D' F#'F#'E'D'E'

F#'F#'F#'F#' D'A D'D' E'E'D'A

ABC#D'D'D' E'F#'G'G' E'C#D'

Drums

A G'G'G' G' F#'E'E' AF#'F#'E'F#'D'

BB C#D' BA D'D' D'D' F#'F#''E'D'E'

F#'F#'F#'F#'F#' D'A D'D' E'E'D'A

ABC#D'D'D' E'F#'G'G' E'C#D'

Brigadier

GABCBABAG GABE'CD' E'F#'G'F#'G'E'D' D'E'D'D'BA
GABCBABAG GABE'CD' E'F#'G'F#'G'E'D'BG CCBAG
E'F#'G'F#'G'E'D' D'E'D'D'BD' E'F#'G'F#'G'E'D'
D'E'D'D'BA
GABCBABAG GABE'CE' E'F#'G'F#'G'E'D'BG CCBAG

I Belong to Glasgow
F#EDEF#GAD' D'E'D'BA F#EDEF#GABC#D'
E'D#'E'F#'E'
AD'E'F#'E'D'E'C#A ABC#D'AF#E
AD'D'D'C#BABAF#GA BC#D'E'D'C'D'

To Make you feel my love

GGGFEG DD GGGFEFcc

FFEEDDE cc ccEccac

CC BB AAGcc EEFEDD cc

CC BB AAGC E Cddeedd

NB. All F's are natural i.e cover holes 1,2,3,4,5 and f key

Young May Moon

Intro D'BCD' BCB AGED D'BCD'BE'D' BAGA

1. DGG DEDD DGGAGABGG

BCC BBABAGF#E F#ED bc# D EDD

2. D'E'E'D'BG E'E'D' D'E'E'D'BGF#AA

D'E'E'D'CBAG F#ED EF#G ABCB GG

Mario Brothers

E'E'E' CE'G' G

CGE GBA#A G E'G'A' F#' G' E'CD'B

CGE GBA#A G E'G'A' F#' G' E'CD'B

G'F#'F' D#E' G#AC ACD'

G'F#'F' D#E' C'C'C'

G'F#'F' D#E' G#AC ACD' D#D'C/ repeat

CCC CD'E'CAG CCCD'E'

CCC CD'E'CAG E'E'E' CE'G' G

CGE GBA#A G E'G'A' F#' G' E'CD'B

CGE GBA#A G E'G'A' F#' G' E'CD'B

E'CG G#A F'F' A BA'A'A' G'F'E' CAG

E'CG G#A F'F' A BF'F'F'E'D'C c / REPEAT

CCC CD'E'CAG CCCD'E'

CCC CD'E'CAG E'E'E' CE'G' G

E'CG G#A F'F' A BA'A'A' G'F#'E' CAG

E'CG G#A F'F' A BF'F'F'E'D'C c

CGE GB A#A G# A# G# G

Farewell to the Creeks

BCD'D' CB A G

G' D' BBABCD'E'D' CBCD'GBD'D'CBA

G' D' BBABCD'E'D' CBCD'D' CB A G

E'D'BD'E'G' F#'E'BE'D'BG BABCD' BCBCA

E'D'BD'E'G' F#'E'BE'D'BG BCD'D' CB A G

G'B C E'BD' BBAG CE'BD'D'CBA

G'B C E'BD' BBAG BCD'D' CB A G

D'G'D'EG' D' E'D'BG CE'BD'D'CBA

D'G'D'EG' D' E'D'BG BCD'D' CB A G

When the Roll is Called up Yonder

GABBB BBAGABGEGD GABBBBD'BAGA

GABBB BBAG ABGEGD GABBAGAAGF#G

BCD' CBCD' B ABC BABC A

BCD' BAGE C GABBB AG AAGF#G

Hallelujah

F#ABB BAF#F# F#ABB BAF#GF#E c#D

AAA F#ABBB AA D'D' C#C#BB

F# BBB BBAAGAA

F#GAAA F#ABBC# C#D'D'D' BC#D'D'E'

C#D'E'E'E'E'F#'F#'F#'E'E'D'

F#ABB BAF#F# F#ABB BAF#GF#E c#D

The Rose

GAB BCBBAA AG GABB GAB BCBBAA AG GABB

BCD'D'D'D'D' GG BC BAGF# GAB BCBBAA AG GAGG

Bonnie English Rose

F'E'D' AF#A F#'E'D'

F#'E'D' AF#A BD'D' C#BA D'F#'D'E'

F#'E'D' AF#A BD'D' C#BA D'F#'E'D'

D'C#D'E' C#D'C#D'E'F#'

D'C#C# D'E'F#' E'

F#'E'D' AF#A BD'D' C#BA D'F#'E'D'

La Montanara

DGBE'D DGBE'D'

DDGG BB E'D' GE'D' G CBA

DDF#F#A A D'D' D'E'D' CBAG

DGBE'D GE'D E'F#'E'

CD'E'D'CD' BD'CA BG

GGABB GAG EF#ED

DF# A CC AD'CBD'

BBCD'D' BE'D'E'F#'E'

CD'E'D'CD' BD'CA BG

Squirrel up a Tree

DEF#F#F#F#F#F#ED EF# GGGGGG AB D'

C#C#C#C# C#C#BAGF#ED F#ABA F#

DEF#F#F#F#F#F#ED EF# GGGGGG AB D'

C#C#C#C# C#C#BAGF#ED F#A F#'E'D'

D'E'F#'F#'F#'F#' F#'G'F#'E'D' C# BAAAA BAF#A

D'C#C#C#C# C#C# BAGF#ED F#ABA F#

D'E'F#'F#'F#'F#' F#'G'F#'E'D' C# BAAAA BAF#A

D'C#C#C#C# C#C# BAGF#ED F#A F#'E'D'

The Corn Reels

D G GAC BAGF#EF#GA F#D

GF#G AB CABG D'D'

D GF#GAC BAGF#EF#GA F#D

E#F#G F# AGF#ED GG

DG D'BCD' F#EF#GAF#D

G D'CBC AB G D'D' BD'E'D'CBCBAGAGF#ED

GF#G AGF#ED GG

Captain Lanoe's Quick March

D' GBD' D'G'F#'E'D' D'CC BB AGAB

BGBD' D'G'F#'E'D' D' CD'C B GAG F#G

GBB BBC BCD' CBAB GBB BBC

BCD' CB GAGF#G

The Stool of Repentence

D'G'D'B D'G'F#'E'D'CB G'E'E'E' DE'G'F#'E'

D'G'D'B D'G'F#'E'D'CB CD'E' D'E'G'BA

GBGG D'GG BGG D'CB

CAA E'AA CACE'D'C

BGG D' GG BGBD'C BCD'E' D'E'G'BA

Farewell to Whisky

DG ABCB ABGEE DG ABCB ABD'BB

E'F#'GF#'E'D'B CBAGA

AB DGABAG BGG

BD'B G'F#'G'E'F#'G'F#'E'D'B

D'B G'F#'G'E'F#'G'

E'F#'G'F#'E'D'B CBAGA

AB DGABAG BGG

The Woodchoppers

DF#AD'BA DF#A D' BA

ac# EGAC#E'G' A'G'E'C#AGF#E

DF#AD'BA DF#A D' BA

ac# EGAC#E'F#' G'E'C#E'D' /1ST AF#/ 2NDF#'G'

A'F#'D'BABAF# DF#AD'F#'E'F#'

G'E'C#BA E'F#'G'A'G#' A'B'A'F#'G'

A'F#'D'BABAF# DF#AD'F#'E'F#'

G'E'C#BA C#E'F#'G' E'C#E'D' / 1STF#G

The Redesdale Hornpipe

D'E'F#'G' D'BD'G D'E'F#'G'D'BD'G

GABC AF#AD ACD'E'D'C#D'B

D'E'F#'G' D'BD'G D'E'F#'G'D'BD'G

GABC AF#AD F#A BA BAGF#G

GABGF#GD GF#G BGF#GD

ABCAF#AD ABCE'D'C#D'B

GABGF#GD GF#G BGF#GD

ABCAF#AD F#ABA BAGF#G

The Banks of the Dee

GDEF#GABC E'D'CBA

BGED D'CBCAG

GDEF#GABC E'D'CBA

BGED D'CBCAG

GABCD'C G'E'D'E'D'BG

BCD'E'F#'G' GAGF#ED

CE'CBD' BGF#GAF# D

GF#ED D'CBCAG

Swaggering Boney

D'BAGABD'E'F#'E'E'

F#'G'F#'G'E' A'G'F#'E'F#'G'

D'BAGABD'E'F#'E'E'

F#'G'F#'G'E' A'G'F#'E'F#'G'

G'A'F#'D' A'F#'D' A'F#'D'D'

BCD'E'E'F#'E' CABC

CBCD'G GCD'E'A

ABCD'E' A'G'F#'E'F#'G'

Sukiyaki

DGG ABGED GGABGED

GGAB GBD'E'E' D'E'D'BA

GGEA ABAGB BAG GGE'D'BGEG

The Queens Delight

D'G'D' CBCBCA BCD'GD'CBCAG

D'G'D' CBCBCA BCD'GD'CBCAG

CBCC BCABCD'E'F#'G'F#'G'E'A'G'G'F#'E'D'

E'F#'G'G'G'F#'E'D'E'CABCD'G D' CBCAG

Roxburgh Castle

BAGF#GBD'BG BCBCE'D'BG

BC E'D'C B G' AABA

C BAGF#GBD'BG BCBCE'D'

BG BD'GF#'G'E'D'CBA BGG

D'G'D'BD'E'D'BD'G'D'BD'E'D'BD'

CA' BG' AABA C BAGF#GBD'BG BCBCE'D'

BG BD'GF#'G'E'D'CBA BGG

Robertson's Reel

GABABD' BAGAGED GABABD' BGBA

GABABD' BAGAGED GABABD'AGF# D'G

BCD'BD'G' F#'G' E'D'BCD'

BCD'BD'G' F#'G' E' D'E'G' GG

BAGAGED GABABD'AGF# D'G

The Haughs of Cromdale

BGEE BGEE BGEEF# DEF#

GG AABD'G EE BGEE

ABE'E' D'G'E' D'E'BD'ABD'

BE'E' D'G'E' D'AF# D'F#EE

The Lonesome Boatman

BABE F#EDE EF#G ABAGF#

BBABE F#ED b EF#G ABAGF# F#EDE F#EDE

B D' E'D'BD' GAB D' E' G'E'D'E' D' BAG

ABAGF# F#EDE F#EDE

Port of Amsterdam

EG AA BC CBABBGE CDE'D'CD CBAAGA

EG AA BC CBABBGE CDE'D'CD CBAAGA

GCC D'E' FE'D'D'CD' CD' E'D'CC BC D' CBBGE

EG AA BC CBABBGE CDE'D'CD CBAAGA

Fleet A Float

D' GGGAGBD'G'E'CD' D' GGGAG BD'E'D'CBA

D'BGGGAG BD'G'G'E'CD' G'E'CD'C AG

BCD'BAB GB D'E'D'BD' BD'E'D'E'G'E'D'BD'E'D'BGA

E'D' BCBAB GB D'E'D'BG' GAB G'D'B ABGG

GBD' GBG' GBD'E'D'BD' GBD' GBG' GBE'D'BGA

E'D' BCBAB GB D'E'D'BG' GAB G'D'B ABGG

Ring of Fire

D'D'D'D' D'E'BD' BBBB BC AB

D'C#D'E'BD' BBB CAB

D' C#D'E'BD' CB B BBAAG

BD' G' G'G' E'E'E' D'B

B D' G'G'G' E'E'E' D'B

BAG BD' BCABD' ABF#G

Game of Thrones

BE GAB E GAF# .....AD GF#A D GF#E

BE GAB E GAF# .....AD GF#A D GF#E

BE GAB E GAF# .....AD F#GF#DE

E'...D'....E...B...c G A B

E'...D'....E...B...c G F# E

Suppliers of B Flat Flutes and Drums

www.ferrismusic.co.uk

Yakumo's Theme

EGA ABA BAGAB D'D'E'B BD'A AGAGG A B

EGA ABA BAGAB D'D'E'B D'BA GABA EEGG

BD'E' E'E'BD' D'CBA G ACB B

BD'E' E'E'E'F#' BD' D' E' GGGEGE'D'

EGA GABA GAB D'D'E'B BD'A AGAG BAG A B

EGA ABA BAGAB D'D'E'B D'BA D'BA EEGG

Hey, Johnnie Cope

EGAAABD'E' AA   GF#GGGABCD'E'DCB

AG CCE'E' CE'G'B   AGE G'E'D'CBAA

C CCCGEG CD'E'F'G' D'CBG D'G BCD'E'D'

CBCBCD'E'D'E' A'G'E'D'CB AGE G'E'D'CBA A

Play with Star of County Down

Wherever You Are

ACF' A'F'E'C F'EC D'CB C

GGCGF cDEGGEc

cDE GGC C E'E' E'E'F'D'CD'

GGCGF cDEGGEc

cDE GGCC E'E' E'E'F'E'CD'

E'E'F'G' CA F'A'G'F'G'

E'GF CC E'E' F'D' CE'F'D'CD'

E'E'F'G' CA F'A'G'F'G'

E'G F' CC GACC G F'E' C D' C

Coming Through the Rye

DDD D' BABD' DDED G

DD D'B AGAB DDED G

D'BGB AGAB D'BGBD'E'

G'D' BC AB GA B DDED G

Above: Peter Worrell Covered Key Crown Flute

Big Rock Candy Mountain

DGGE DGGE DGGAGABD'

DGGE DGGE DGGAGABD'

D'E'E'D' G E'E'D' D'E'D'CBAD

DGG E DGGE DGGAGABG

BAGGG ABD' BD'E'E'G'G'D'

BD'E'E' G'G'D'D'D' BE'D'CBA

BAGGG ABD' BD'E'E'G'G'D'

BD'E'E'D' BD'E'E'E'D' BD'E'E'D'

 BD'E'E'E'D' BCD'D'D' BAG

Gallowa Hills

D'B GGG ABBB CD'G'D'

BCCC AFFF AC F'E'D'

BCD'D'D' BGGG BD'G'D'

BG CBC E'D' BA F#G

The Bonnie Lass of Fyvie O'

D GF#G AG D GF#G AG

D GBCD' CBA DD

D' BABCD' D GAGE cbc

D GAGF#ED GAG

Old Joe Clarke

ABC#D'C#BAG# ABC#D'C#B

ABC#D'C#BAG# E G#G#F# DE

EE ABAG# G#GF# DE

EE ABAG# EG#G#F#DE

Blue Nose

F# BC#D'C#BABEF# F#BC#D'D'C#D'E'

E'E'F#'G'E'F#' D'C#D'E'C#D'

C#BD'C#BC#C#BAB F#BC#C#D'E'D'C#B

BD'C#BAEF# F#BC#C#D'E'D'C#B

F#'G'F#'E'D'C#BAB

Nancy Whiskey

GG BBA GF#D GG BD' BAG

GF#GABB ABA GF#D

GF#G ABB D'E'E'D'

D'B G' D'BGED GAB AGED

Mason's Lane

DEG G' BAGABAGE DEG G' BAGA

DEG G' BAGABAGE DEG G' BAG

BCD' G'F#'G' BCD'E'D'BD'

BCD' G'F#'G' BD'

BCD' G'F#'G' BCD'E'D'BD'

BAG D' BAG

Ardoyne

ABAF#F#EF#A D'D' BBAB BC#D'D'C#D'BA AB EEF#E

ABA F#F#EF#A D'D'BBAB BC#D'D'C#D'BA EF#GGF#ED

D'E'D' BBABD' G'G'E'E'D'E' E'F#'G'G'F#'G'E'D' C#D'E'AABA D'E'D' BBABD' G'G'E'E'D'E'

E'F#'G'G'F#'G'E'D' C#D'E' E'F#'F#'G'

Pistroli

DDEF#AA BD'F#'D'E'D'B

AA BD'F#' A'F#'E'D'E'F#'E'E'

DDEF#AA BD'F#'D'E'D'B

AA BD'F#'A' F#'E'D'E'F#'E'D'D'

F#'AA BAF#D'E' F#D'E'F#'D'BA

F#DEF# ABAB D'E' D'F#'D'E' E'

F#'AA BAF#D'E' F#D'E'F#'D'BA

F#DEF# ABAB D'E' D'F#'E'E'D'D'

Menin Gate

AABD'D' E'F#'G'F#'E'D'F#' D'D'D'C#D'BA GF#G

AA BD'D' E'F#'G'F#'E'D'F#' E'E'E'D'E'F#'E' AF#G

AA BD'D' E'F#'G'F#'E'D'F#' D'D'D'C#D'E'F#'

F#'G'F#'BG'G'F#'G'A' AF#'F#'E'F#'G' E'D'C#BC#D'E'D'

G'D'D'CBCD'B E'BBAGF#GAG ABCD'G'F#'E' B A G

AABD'D' E'F#'G'F#'E'D'F#' D'D'D'C#D'E'F#'

F#'G'F#'BG'G'F#'G'A' AF#'F#'E'F#'G' E'D'C#BC#D'E'D'

D' G'D'D' CBC D' B E' BBAGF#AGABCD' G'F#'E' B A G

AA BD'D' E'F#'G'F#'E'D'F#' D'D'D'C#D'E'F#'

F#'G'F#'BG'G'F#'G'A' AF#'F#'E'F#'G' E'D'C#BC#D'E'D'

Red Mountain Jig

D'E'F#'D'A GF#G E'C#A E#'

AE'C#A D'C# BABAF#GA

F#'D'A GF#G E'C#A E#' A E'C#A

D'C# BA BC#D'

AF#EF#DEF# GF#GE

D'C#BC# ABC#D'C#BA

AF#EF#DEF#GF#GE

D'C#BC#A F#'E'D'

Servant King

D'D'CB BBAG GABC BAGB

D'D'CB GABBCD'E' G'G'E'D' BBAG

BBCBAGE ABCD' GCBA

BBCBAGE ABCD' GCBA

D'D'CB BBAG GABC BAGB

D'D'CB GABBCD'E' G'G'E'D' BBAG

Balquidder Lasses

BAG EE F#GABB E' BD' AABAF#DEF#GA

BAG EE F#GABB E' BD' ABAGF#EE

BAG EE F#GABB E' BD' AABAF#DEF#GA

BAG EE F#GABB E' BD' ABAGF#EE

B E'D#'E'F#'E' B E'F#'G'F#'E'

BC#D'D'D' BAF# DEF#GA

B E'D#'E'F#'E' B E'F#'G'F#'E'

BC#D' ABAGF#EE

B E'D#'E'F#'E' B E'F#'G'F#'E'

BC#D'D'D' BAF# DEF#GA

BAG F#GE F#GABB E' BD' ABAGF#EE

Brian Robinson

AGF# EF#A F#'E'D' F#GF#GAB

E'E'F#'E'D'D'C# C#BA A BAGF#

AGF# EF#A F#'E'D' F#GF#GAB

E'E'F#'E'D'D'C# C#BA AA G'F#'E'D'

Highfield Drive

F#'D' A D'E'F#'F#'G'F#'E'D'

E'C#A C#D'E'E'F#'G'F#'E'

F#'D' A D'E'F#'F#'G'F#'E'D'

E'E' F#'G'G'F#'E'D'

BGD GABBCBAG

AF#D F#GAA BCBA

BGD GABBCBAG

 AA BCCBAG

All Over Europe

AA D'F#'G'F#'E'F#'D' AD' F#'F#'F#'G'F#'E'

D'C#D'E'D'E'F#'E'C# ABA G'F#'E'F#'

AA D'F#'G'F#'E'F#'D' AD' F#'F#'F#'G'F#'E'

D'C#D'E'D'E'F#'E'C# ABA G'F#'E'D'

Wolverhampton Town

D'B D'CB ABAGG ED DGF#GABBAGA D'E'D'

D'B D'CB ABAGGED DGGG ABBAF#G

Farewell to Nova Scotia

CD'E'D' CBC BAGE ABA

GCBC D'C EFGGAG CBA BCD'E' ABA

CD'E'E'D'CD' D'BGF#GBD' CD'E'D' CBC BAGE ABA

That Sacred Spot

D GG AGF#D GAB AABAGF#GABC

ABD'C BACB G AABA GF#EF#ED

DBBB BCBAGA ECCC CD'CBAG

BD'D'B BAA GE C F#ED c#D G BAEF#G

BA#B D'CBAG#A AG#A CBAGF#G

GG AGF#D GAB ABAGF#GABC

BA#B D'CBAG#A AG#A CBAGF#G

GG AGF#D GAB BCD'E'D'CBAG

When Pipers Play

D GAB AGED DGF#G GABC A

ABCD' CBAGB AGED DEGF#G

GABC ABCD' D'BGGA

DDCB BAGAB AGED DEG F#G

Bad Romance

D'E'F#'G'G'F#'G'F#'E'

C#D'E'F#'F#'E'F#'E'D'

D'E'F#'G'G'F#'G'F#'E'

C#D'E'F#'F#'E'F#'E'D'

BB F#'F#'G'F#' BBB F#'F#'G'F#'

BB F#'F#' G#' BBBF#'F#'G'F#'

BBBC# BC#D'BABA

BBBC# BC#D' BAB

F#ABB F#'E'D' F#ABB

The Massacre of Glencoe

D BAG EF#G EcED DBAG DGF#A

BAG EF#G EcED DED GF#GAAG

DGB GAC ABD' BD BAC AD BBC BA

DGB GAC ABD'BD DED GF# GAAG

The Pansy Blossom

BCD'G'D'BD'BGBGD b DGBD'BG

BCE'CA CAF#AF#D ABAGF#ED

BCD'G'D'BD'BGBGD b DGABCD'E'F#'

G'F#'E'D'CB F#'E'D'CBA GAB DEF#G

ABCAF#AD F#ABC AF#A C

BCD'BGBGD GBCD' BGBD'G'

F#'G' E'F#'E' D'E'D' CD'C BCB GABC D'E'

D'E'F#'G'F#'E'D'CBF#'E'D'CBA GAB DEF#G

Look at the Coffin

D'D'C#D' BAG G'G'F#'G'E'D'C   CCD'E'D'B BBBAGA

D'D'C#D' BAG E'E'E'CD'E'D' D' E'E'E'G'F#' E'D'E'D'

B E'D'E'D''CBAG

Sweet Sixteen

AF#D F#A D'F#'E'D'B GGEG C#E' D'C#D'A

AF#D F#A D'F#'E'D'B BBC#E'C#BA

A D'E'F#' AF#'G' E' D'D'

Morrison's Jig

EEE BEB EEE AF#D EEE BEB D'C#BAF#D

EEE BEB EEE AF#D GG F#GAD' AF#ED

EEE BEB EEE AF#D EEE BEB D'C#BAF#D

EEE BEB EEE AF#D GG F#GAD' AF#ED

BE'E'F#'E'E' A'E'E'F#'E'D'

BE'E'F#'E'E' A' G'F#'E'D'

BE'E'F#'E'E' A'E'E'F#'E'E'

G'F#E'D'A BAGF#GA

BE'E'F#'E'E' A'E'E'F#'E'D'

BE'E'F#'E'E' F#'A'F#' D'E'F#'G'

G'G' F#'E'D'E'F#'G' D'E'D'

C#D' ABAGF#ED

Above: Miller Wicks Crown

Leaning on the Everlasting Arms

Intro/
BBBAG AAAGE DD GF#GAB AG

BBBAG AAAGE DD GF#GABBA

BBBAG AAAGE DD GF#GAB AG

BG GE DDEG BBA

BG GE DD GF#GAB AG

Spanish Lady

DDDEF#GGGAB CAB GE DD

DDDEF#GGGAB CAB GE DD

BD'D'D' BAGABCD'D'D' BAGA

BD'D'D' BAGA ABC ABGEDD

DDDEF#GGGAB CAB GE DD

DDDEF#GGGAB CAB GE DD

Londonderry Air

a DEF# EF# BAF#EDb DF#GA BAF#DF#E

a DEF# EF# BAF#EDb DDEF# GF#EDED

ABC#D' D'C# BA BAF# D ABC#D' D'C# BAF#E

AAA F#' E'E'D' BD' AF# D DDEF# BAF#E Dbc#D

Donegal Danny

DB CB AGED DEG AGGED

D D'D'D' CBAG GABCBAGA

BAGGGABCE'D' BD'D' CBAGA

BAGGG ABCD'E'D' E'D'CBAGF#GAB

E'D' CBAGF#G

Mc Gregor's March 02/186

E AA BCABAG DGG ABD'BAG

E AA BCAB E'D'B G' BAA

E'E'D'CAA GBCD' BAGF#ED

E'E'D'CAA E'D'B G' BAA

Calliope House

E'C#E'E' BE'E' ABC#D' C#D'C# BC#B

BAF# EF#EE c# EF#ABC#E' C#C#BAB BC#D'

E'C#E'E' BE'E' ABC#D' C#D'C# BC#B

BAF# EF#EE c# EF#ABC#E'C# BAF#AA

EA EEC# EEB EE C#BA F# BBB ABC#BAF#

EF#EE c#EF#ABC#E' C#C#BAB

E'C#E'E' BE'E' ABC#D' C#D'C# BC#B

BAF# EF#EE c# EF#A BC#E' C#BC#BAA

London's Return

D'E'F#'AA D'C#BABD'E' D'E'F#'A G'F#'E'D'B C#D'

D'E'F#'AA D'C#BABD'E' D'E'F#'A G'F#'E'D'BC#D'

D'GABCD' BCBAGF#A D'GABCD' CBGBCD'

D'GABCD' BCBAGF#A GAB D CBAGEF#G

Battle of Culloden Moor

BD'D' G CE'D'G BD'D' G BC BBA

E'D'D'G E'CD'D' G BBCD'D' G GA BA AG

Belvedere

D BCD' BA CBAG G'F#'G'E'

A'G'F#'G'F#'E'D'D#'E'CB E'D' BA

D'CB CBAG G'F#'G'E' D' CBA

A'G'F#'G'F#'E'D' BCAG GGG

AGF#GABC E'D'CBAGF#G

BCD'E'D' CBA A'A'G'F#'GF#'E'D'

D'CB CBAG G'F#'G'E' D' CBA

A'G'F#'G'F#'E'D' BCAG GGG

Loch Roan

GACG G'E' D'CD'E'F'A D'CBAGF'D'BC D'E'G

GACG G'E' D'CD'E'F'A D'CBAGF' D'ABC C D'C

E'F'G'E'CG G'E'CD'E'F'A D'E'F'D'BG F'D'BCD'E'G

E'F'G'E'CG G'E'CD'E'F'A D'CBAGF' D'ABC CD' C

Golden Days

DG DGB GBD'E'D'BGBAGF#DF#AF#AD'CB AG

DEF#G DGB GBD'E'D'BG GFF#E c EGF# GAF#G GG

FEcE GAGEG Dc#D GG BAGF#EF#ACAF#AGF#GAB

GF#FEcE GAGEG Dc#D GG

BAGF#EF#ACAF#AG GAG

Promoting The Band Scene

www.bandparades.co.uk

McNamara's Band

D' CBBB BBBB BBBB AGD

CCC CBBB BAGF#GA

D' C BBB BBBB BBBBAGD

CCBAD' BGED CBAG

DEF#G E'D'BA E BAGF# D'C#D'E'D' BAB

BD'D'D'D' D'CBA D'D'D'D' BCBA BCD' B CCCBAG

Carson's Call

E CCCCB CBAGA AGEE EEAGF

FBBBBA AAGGG FFFFFEDE

E CCCCB CBAGA AGEE EFEF

F D'D'D'D' C BBAGG AGFFFGABC

EGCE'E'CG FAGG EGCE'E'CG FAG

BBBB BCB F'F'F'F'E' GGGG GGG GABE'D'C

The Riddle

BC#D'D'E'D'C#BA A BC#C#

BC#D'D'E'D'C# BA BBAA

BC#D'D'E'D'C#BA A BC#C#

BC#D'D'E'D'C# BA BBAA

F#'A'G'F#'E'D'B ABB

BD'E'E'D' BB D'CBAGB

E'D'CBD'E'ED' BBD'CBAGE

D'E'D'

A Dying Soldiers Words

GABBB AAG D'E'G'F#'E'D'

D'E'F#G'F#'E'D' GABD'CBA

GABBB AAG D'E'G'F#'E'D'

D'E'F#G'F#'E'D'B GABBBAG

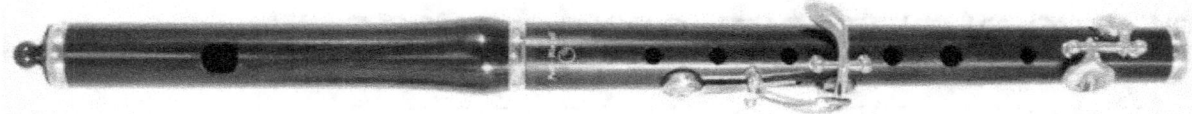

Above, A Peter Worrell two piece , three key Crown

Goodbye Mursheen Durkin

GABBAGAD' E'F#'D'BAAG

GABBAGAD' E'F#' D'E'F#'G'

DG'G'A' G'F#'D' E'F#'D' BAAG

GABBAGAD' E'F#'D'E'F#'G'

The Muckin of Geordie's Byre

CAGAGG EGAC G'F' D'E' CD' CABC

GAGG EGAC E'G'E'C D'E'D'CC

CD'E'F'F'F' G'F'E'E'E' G'E'D'D'DE'F'E' CABC

GAGGEGAC E'G'E'C D'E'D'CC

Campbell's Farewell to Redcastle

D' GAB C'D'G'D' CBGG ABC CAF

AG ABCD'G'D' CB AGFGA FGG

F'E'D' G'G' F'E'D' G'D' CBGGABC CAF

F'E'D' G'G' F'E'D' G'D' CBAGF GAFGG

F'E'D' G'G' F'E'D' G'D' CBGGABC CAF

DGABC BCD'E' D'E'F'G'D' D' CBAGFGA FGG

The Heights of Dargai

D'GABD' B D'E'BE'D' B

G'F#'E'D' B D'E'D'BAA

D'GABD' B D'E'BE'D' B

G'F#'E'D'A CBCAGG

GBCE'E'C E'G'F#'E'D'B

G'F#'E'D' A D'E'D'BAA

GBCE'E'C E'G'F#'E'D'B

G'F#'E'D' A CBCAGG

Brochan Lom

D' CB GGF#G DGGF#G BGD'BG

ABC AABAF#AABA F#EAF#D

D' CB GGF#G DGGF#G BGD'BG

BCD'E' CD' BC AB AGF#EF#G

D' CB D'D'C#D' BD'D'C#D' BCD'BG

ABCE'E'D'E'CE'E'D'E'CD'E'CA

D' CB D'D'C#D' BD'D'C#D' BCD'BG

BCD'E' CD' BC AB AGF#EF#G

Devil Among the Tailors

ABD' ABD' ABD' AD'BAGFGBE

BGBE B BABC#D'C#BA

D'ABD' ABD' AD'BAGF#

BAGF# GF#ED c ED

AGF#AD AF#AD AF#A DABAGF#

GBE BGBE B BABC#D'C#BA

AGF#AD AF#AD AF#A DABAGF#

BAGF# GF#ED cED

AGF#AD AF#AD AF#A DABAGF#

EEEF#GF#G ABABC#D'C#BA

AGF#AD AF#AD AF#A DABAGF#

BAGF# GF#ED cED

AGF# DDEDDDc#DDDEF#

ED GEEF#EEED EF#GAB

AGF# DDEDDDc#DDDEF#

ED GF#G ABAB D' AGF#ED

Devil Among the Tailors (Cont'd)

AGF#D ADBDAD F#D ADBD AD

GEBE D'EBE GE BED'EBE

F#D ADBDAD F#D ADBD AD

GF#GABAB D' AGF#ED

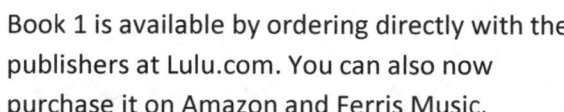

Book 1 is available by ordering directly with the publishers at Lulu.com. You can also now purchase it on Amazon and Ferris Music.

If you are a retail outlet and interested in stocking the books please get in touch for more information.

The first Book has over 300 tunes and features more of the traditional tunes that have been popular with many bands over the years .

www.ingramcontent.com/pod-product-compliance
Lightning Source LLC
Chambersburg PA
CBHW081201280526
45789CB00006B/2262